MARCUS BRAYBROO

A HEART
FOR THE WORLD

FOREWARD BY HANS KUNG

MARCUS BRAYBROOKE

A HEART
FOR THE WORLD

THE INTERFAITH ALTERNATIVE

With best wishes

Marcus Braybrooke

BOOKS

WINCHESTER UK
NEW YORK USA

First published 2005 by O Books
O Books is an imprint of John Hunt Publishing Ltd., The Bothy,
Deershot Lodge, Park Lane, Ropley, Hants, SO24 0BE, UK
office@johnhunt-publishing.com
www.O-books.net

Distribution in:
UK
Orca Book Services
orders@orcabookservices.co.uk
Tel: 01202 665432 Fax: 01202 666219 Int. code (44)

USA and Canada
NBN
custserv@nbnbooks.com
Tel: 1 800 462 6420 Fax: 1 800 338 4550

Australia
Brumby Books
sales@brumbybooks.com
Tel: 61 3 9761 5535 Fax: 61 3 9761 7095

New Zealand
Peaceful Living
books@peaceful-living.co.nz
Tel: 64 7 57 18105 Fax: 64 7 57 18513

Singapore
STP
davidbuckland@tlp.com.sg
Tel: 65 6276 Fax: 65 6276 7119

South Africa
Alternative Books
altbook@global.co.za
Tel: 27 011 792 7730 Fax: 27 011 972 7787

Text: © Marcus Braybrooke 2005

Design: BookDesign™, London, UK

ISBN 1 905047 43 6

A CIP catalogue record for this book is available from the
British Library.

Printed in the USA by Maple-Vail Manufacturing Group

DEDICATION

*To all my family, my friends in the interfaith
family and to the parishioners of Marsh Baldon,
Toot Baldon and Nuneham Courtenay, thank you
for all your encouragement and support.*

CONTENTS

FOREWORD

Marcus Braybrooke is a witness of our times. He has participated in the whole long development of interfaith dialogue in the 20th century. He has published a number of books and a lot of articles, has actively participated in many conferences and has tackled issues of our world and of religions on the intellectual level. I appreciate especially his deep involvement in the Parliaments of the World's Religions and his commitment to a Global Ethic. But Marcus is equally a grassroots activist: as a minister of the Church he has always struggled for realizing his concerns in pastoral work.

This book is therefore not a treatise or theory but a document of life experience. It is especially precious in a time when many people tend to despair: indeed, the hope for universal peace, nurtured fifteen years ago, has considerably diminished, many politicians have disappointed the people, innumerous financial and political scandals have shocked the world, and the religions and their representatives have not always played a role conducive to peace. In such a time encouragement is needed, and Marcus Braybrooke draws it from concrete examples of practices where people have committed themselves to the cause of peace and justice and shown a heart for the world.

I strongly hope that this book may be contagious by sowing hope and stimulating action.

Tübingen, March 2005   Hans Küng

PREFACE

It was in 1964 that I joined the World Congress of Faiths. Despite some remarkable pioneers, interfaith co-operation was in its infancy and viewed with suspicion both by most religious leaders and academic scholars in the Study of Religions.

Today, interfaith activity occurs in many countries at a local and national level and, thanks to a number of international interfaith organisations, it also has a global dimension. Increasingly, political and business leaders are recognizing its importance, but the comparative popularity of interfaith activity may mask the radical alternative and challenge that it offers to our entrenched ways of thinking about religion, violence, economics and the environment.

The aim of this book is to highlight this alternative vision and to suggest ways in which it can be translated into practical policies that will help to create a "Civilization with a Heart".

Once again, I would like to thank all my colleagues in the interfaith movement, especially friends in the World Congress of Faiths, the Three Faiths Forum, the Peace Council, the International Interfaith Centre and the Parliament of Religions. I am particularly grateful to Professor Hans Kung and Sir Sigmund Sternberg for messages of encouragement. I am also grateful for all the support I received from my parishioners at Marsh Baldon, Toot Baldon and Nuneham Courtenay, and to members of the Dorchester-on-Thames Team ministry near Oxford. My thanks go to John Hunt and all involved in the publishing of this book. Once again I want to say a special thank you to my family for their interest and, of course, to Mary in particular for her unfailing encouragement and active participation in this work. It was in 1964 also that I married and that I was ordained.

Although I deal with issues that are complex, I hope the argument is clear. To this end, I often do not mention in the text the names of those scholars to whose work I am indebted, but their names are given in the notes, which I trust will be of particular use to students and to those who want to follow up points of interest.

My friend Wayne Teasdale, a pioneer of inter-spirituality, died a few months before I finished this book. I hope it will contribute to the fulfilment of his dream that the mystics would lead the way to a "rebirth of the human community that will harmonize itself with the cosmos and finally make peace with all beings".[1]

April 2005

---

1 Wayne Teasdale, *The Mystic Heart*, New World Library, Novato, California, 1999, p.250

INTRODUCTION

It is no wonder that many people are turned off by religion. So often it is a cause of division and violence. Terrible atrocities, such as the brutal killing of innocent children at Beslan, are perpetrated supposedly in the name of God.   But, as Rabbi Hugo Gryn, a survivor of the concentration camps, said of Auschwitz, the question is not, "Where was God?" but "Where was man?"[1]

This book is not a defence of God. Instead, it is a call to believers, in a violent and greedy world, to reclaim the core values of their faith, to proclaim them clearly and to live by them. Only if we are willing to sacrifice ourselves and put other people first, as every religion teaches, will we reverse the cycle of violence, begin to close the ever widening gap between rich and poor and preserve the planet from environmental disaster.

But judgment begins with the house of God. Religious people need to acknowledge with penitence that religion itself has too often fostered prejudice and exclusivism, which can lead to hatred, and that they have colluded with economic injustice.

A small, but growing, number of people, drawn from all faiths, have turned their back on religious rivalry and, impatient with institutional religion, are working together for a more just and peaceful world. In 1993, thousands of people gathered in Grant Park

---

1 Hugo Gryn, *Chasing Shadows*, Viking, 2000, p. 251

in Chicago, for the culmination of a Parliament of Religions. After short prayers from many religious traditions and an address by the Dalai Lama, a *Declaration Toward A Global Ethic* was read. This made clear the essential agreement on moral values that exists among members of different religions and provides the basis for people of faith to act together to transform our world society.

The Parliament was a highpoint in what is known as the interfaith movement, which had begun one hundred years earlier at the World's Parliament of Religions, held in Chicago in 1893. Of course, in much of Asia and elsewhere, members of different faiths had lived together for centuries, sometimes amicably, sometimes with one group discriminating against others, sometimes with active hostility. At the Parliament, however, some people, such as the Hindu Swami Vivekananda, recognized that there is truth in every religion, which means that people of different faiths are not rivals but partners in the service of God and of the world. The President of the Parliament, Charles Bonney, said, "when the religious faiths of the world recognize each other as brothers, children of one Father, whom all profess to love and serve, then, and not till then, will the nations of the earth yield to the Spirit of concord and learn war no more."[2]

As participants left Chicago in 1893, after what the scholar Max Müller described as "one of the most memorable events in the history of the world",[3] they talked of holding another Parliament in India in 1900. It was not until one hundred years later that the Parliament met again. The twentieth century, which was dominated by the rise of Communism and Fascism - both of which were hostile to religion - was a century of appalling bloodshed and genocide. Even so, the dream of 1893 did not disappear and small groups such as the International Association for Religious Freedom (IARF) and the World Congress of Faiths (WCF) kept alive the hope that religious people could work together for a better world. Many of

---

2 Charles Bonney in *The World's Parliament of Religions*, ed. John Henry Barrows, Chicago 1893, p. 67.
3 Max Müller, 'The Real Significance of the Parliament of Religions', Arena 11, December 1894, pp. 1-2, quoted in Marcus Braybrooke, *Pilgrimage of Hope*, SCM Press, London, 1992, p. 7.

these pioneers were on the edge of organized religion and often met with hostility from acknowledged religious leaders. Even so, they broke down ignorance by publications and lectures and dispelled prejudice by encouraging people of different faiths to meet, to talk and often to become friends. As they did this, they also began to question the traditional teaching of their religion about other religions. For example, some Christians could no longer believe that Hindus, Muslims and others, like illegal immigrants, would be turned back at the heavenly portal.

From the beginning, interfaith pioneers did not see inter-religious meetings as an end in themselves, but as a vital contribution to peace and human welfare. As a student in India, I went with another Christian and a Muslim student to help at a leprosy clinic. The doctor was a Hindu. I saw then the possibility that people of all religions could come together to care for the needy. This increasingly is now beginning to happen as people of different faiths, having become friends, have begun to campaign for peace or to help the victims of war and disaster. American Christians and Vietnamese Buddhists, who both opposed the Vietnamese war, found they were allies. In the 'sixties, I got to know Muslims in the Medway Towns when I helped to raise money for the victims of flooding in Bangladesh. The greatest threat to human survival, at the time, was, of course, the proliferation of nuclear weapons and it was opposition to the nuclear menace that brought people of many faiths together to form the World Conference of Religion and Peace in 1970.

Interfaith work, by the 'eighties, was becoming more practical – although some monks and nuns were sharing a deeper spiritual journey. At the same time, leaders of faith communities were becoming more involved and willing to attend meetings arranged by interfaith organisations, although today, such leaders are directly in touch with each other and do not need interfaith organizations as intermediaries.

These developments caught the attention of the public during the centenary year of the 1893 Parliament of Religions, which was celebrated in many places as a Year of Inter-religious Understanding and Co-operation. It was a time also when a wider public was waking up to the dangers of religious extremism and fundamentalism.

In answer to religious conflict in former Yugoslavia, in India and elsewhere, a *Declaration Toward a Global Ethic* was agreed, which affirms the moral values that religions share. The task was now to apply them to a strife-torn and hungry world. This entailed engaging key people in business, education, government, media, science, civil society and religion. To do this, the Parliament developed a *Call to the Guiding Institutions.* At the same time, some members of those institutions were themselves recognizing that there is a spiritual and moral dimension to the great problems that face our world. Multi-faith dialogue was, therefore, becoming multi-disciplinary dialogue. Sadly, the process was not continued at the 2004 Parliament of Religions in Barcelona. Although the 2004 Parliament emphasized four key issues – access to clean water, the plight of refugees, cancellation of the debt of the most impoverished nations, and reducing religiously motivated violence - its focus was on the simple but profound acts that individuals could make to address these concerns. The Parliament did not engage with the powers that be. Nonetheless, as the editors of *Intereligious Insight* declare "the deep dialogue between religions and the other most influential institutions … is one of the most urgent needs of our age."[4]

This engagement is beginning to happen, for example, by the presence of some religious leaders at the World Economic Forum or in the dialogue between the World Bank and religious leaders. It is high on the agenda of the Three Faiths Forum. Some governments are starting to meet with leaders of faith communities and beginning to consult with them. In December 2004, for example, several heads of state in South East Europe agreed the Tirana Declaration on Inter-religious and Inter-ethnic dialogue, which says that "peace is

---

4 *Interreligious Insight,* Vol. 2, No.4, October 2004, p. 7.

indivisible from dialogue," adding "that the challenge we face every single day is to replace fear with acceptance, harassment with tolerance, and hatred with respect.'[5] In several countries politicians have gone out of their way to insist that the war against terror is not a war against Islam. Recently, the United Nations Assembly has affirmed the importance of inter-religious dialogue.

This, therefore, is a time of opportunity, as well as of great danger. But I am afraid that the interfaith movement may miss the moment. Partly this is because international interfaith organisations have failed to get their act together. They remain fragmented and their voice is scarcely heard. More significantly, people of faith have failed clearly to articulate an alternative to present policies which respond to violence with violence and which do nothing to alleviate the suffering of the poor. The ancient wisdom, which is based on the Unitive or Mystic realization of oneness with the Source of Life in whom all are one, is that violence is only overcome by love and that the affluent should make real sacrifices to alleviate the misery of destitute. I fear that having come close to the corridors of power, religious representatives instead of challenging the values and policies of governments may instead be seduced and co-opted by governments.

I do not claim to know detailed answers to the urgent problems that confront our world, but I hope this book will encourage more people to see that the affirmation of religious pluralism and the application of our shared moral values to the problems that confront us does indeed offer a radical alternative to the policies at present being pursued by the major powers. I believe that only a practical spirituality, grounded in the interfaith vision, can ensure hope and life for all humankind.

5 The Tirana Summit Declaration, 10.12.04.

RELIGIOUS DIVERSITY IS A BLESSING

RELIGIOUS DIVERSITY IS A BLESSING

We have a choice

There is an alternative.

Soon after the attack on the twin towers on September 11th, 2001, the Dalai Lama said that two responses were possible to those terrible events. One came from fear, the other from love. "If we could love even those who have attacked us, and seek to understand why they have done so ... we would become spiritual activists".[1] For this to happen, the Dalai Lama said, we need Divine help and mutual support to grow in inner peace and wisdom.

Dr Rowan Williams, the Archbishop of Canterbury, who was in a building close to the twin towers at the time of the attack, also said we have a choice. "When someone 'spoke' to us in violence and murder, we could choose what we should do. We may rightly want to defend ourselves and one another – our people, our families, the weak and vulnerable among us. But we are not forced to act in revengeful ways, holding up a mirror to the terrorist acts done to us. If we do act in the same way as our enemies, we imprison ourselves in their anger, their evil. And we fail to show our belief in the living God who always requires of us justice and goodness".[2]

---

1 Quoted in *The International Interfaith Centre's Newsletter*, Oxford, December 2001.
2 Address of Rowan Williams at Al-Azhar al-Sharif, Cairo, 11.9.04, reproduced in *Westminster Interfaith Newsletter*, Issue 39, November 2004, p.5.

The next day, I was myself contacted by e-mail by someone I did not know who lived in the outskirts of Washington. As he heard the grim news, he returned home and gathered his family and then happened to pick up the copy of my anthology, *Bridge of Stars*, which had arrived that morning. He opened the book and tried to focus his thoughts on this extract from the Jain :

> I give friendship to all and enmity to none.
> Know that violence is the root cause of all miseries in the world.
> Violence, in fact, is the knot of bondage.
> "Do not injure any living being."
> This is the eternal, perennial, and unalterable way of spiritual life.
> A weapon, however powerful it may be,
> Can always be superseded by a superior weapon;
> However no weapon can be superior to non-violence and love.[3]

There is an alternative: to seek reconciliation rather than revenge, to live more simply that others may simply live and to reverence all life with which we share this planet. This alternative is rooted in the conviction that every person is precious to God – that the terrorist as well as his or her victim is God's child. Such teaching is to be found in all the religions, although often it has been obscured. It also flows from the mystic sense of the oneness of all life.

To explain what I mean by this mystic sense of oneness, I will quote from Francis Younghusband's account of his decisive spiritual experience just outside Lhasa in Tibet in 1903. Younghusband probably had no business to be in Tibet and I don't wish to justify this British military adventure. Later in life, however, Younghusband founded the World Congress of Faiths in 1936, which was one of the first interfaith

---

3 Quoted in *Bridge of Stars*, Ed. Marcus Braybrooke, Duncan Baird, 2001, p.197.

organisations and of which I have been a member for forty years. The sense of oneness, of which Younghusband speaks, has motivated my own interfaith work. He wrote:

> "The day after leaving Lhasa, I went off alone to the mountainside … I was beside myself with untellable joy … I felt in touch with the flaming heart of the world … A mighty joy-giving Power was at work in the world – at work in all about me and at work in every living thing. So it was revealed. Never again could I think evil. Never again could I bear enmity. Joy had begotten love."[4]

Rowan Williams put this rather differently. "To seek to find reconciliation, to refuse revenge and the killing of the innocent, this is a form of adoration towards the One Living and Almighty God."[5]

Diversity is a strength not a threat

In the presence of the Eternal Lover, in whom all are one, divisions fade away. The first division that fades is between followers of different religions. Does it matter to God what is our religious label? Surely, when we pray "Lord have mercy upon us", if the "us" means anything less than all humanity, our prayers fall short of the mercy of God.

This means that the first barrier that interfaith work has to break down is defining our religious identity over against other people. At many interfaith conferences, when there are the inevitable small groups, each person is usually asked to introduce herself or himself. "I am a Hindu, I am a Baha'i, I am a Buddhist." It was a refreshing change when someone began, "I am a human being".

4 Francis Younghusbannd, *Vital Religion*, John Murray, 1940, pp.3-4.
5 Address of Rowan Williams at Al-Azhar al-Sharif, Cairo, 11.9.04, reproduced in *Westminster Interfaith Newsletter*, p. 6.

Although a religion may bind its members together, it also distinguishes them from other people. Religion thus becomes intertwined with our sense of identity. It was a shock to me when I first read this passage by the social anthropologist Richard Gombrich:

> For most people in the modern world, religion is first of all an identity, a label, a badge of allegiance of a group. What is your religion? it says on the form, and the terrorist asks the same question. Protestant and Catholic in Ulster, Hindu and Sikh in the Punjab ... In this sense religion cannot be quite separated from politics or indeed from racism.[6]

I realized I had seen "religion" only through Western eyes. Gombrich goes on to say that in defining a religion:

> The first answer that occurs to someone from a Christian background is likely to be that religion is a matter of belief, particularly of belief in God. But half the world does not think in these terms. For them, religion is first and foremost what you do not what you think. A Hindu or a Jew must avoid certain foods.[7]

There is the well-known story of a visitor to Belfast who was asked, "What is your religion?" He replied he was Jewish. "Yes", his questioner persisted, "but are you a Protestant Jew or a Catholic Jew?" I remember also as a national serviceman that almost the first thing I was given was a metal disc to wear around my neck. On it were stamped the letters CE (Church of England). The alternatives were RC (Roman

---

6 R Gombrich, "What Kind of Thing is Religion" in *SHAP Handbook on World Religions in Education*, Commission for Racial Equality, 1987.
7 *Ibid.*

Catholic) and OD (Other Denominations). This meant the army could provide an appropriate funeral if required.

The importance of religion in shaping the community with which a person identifies and therefore in shaping a person's sense of identity is easily underestimated especially by those who live in an increasingly secularized world. Even they, however, if they choose to marry someone from a different religious background, may still be surprised by the strong hostile reaction from older members of the family. In some societies, schooling, health care and family law is determined by the religious community to which a person belongs. Members of different religions or cultural background may live in geographical proximity but there may be no human interaction beyond what is necessary to buy a bus ticket or to pay for the shopping at a supermarket check-out. In Zimbabwe, we were guests of a white couple who considered themselves very liberal. All their immediate neighbors, who were black, belonged to professional classes. My wife asked, "Do you invite some of your neighbors into your house?" "No, it's not something that we have done yet", was the reply. In Oxford, where we live, we asked a woman from Afghanistan, who was serving at a local Supermarket check-out, "How do you like England?" She replied, "No one talks to me".

This is the point made by Samuel P Huntington, well known for his catch phrase, *A clash of civilizations.* In an article, published in 1993, he emphasized "the explosive nature of religion".[8] He wrote:

> Blood, language, religion, way of life were what the Greeks had in common and what distinguished them from the Persians and other non-Greeks. Of all the objective elements which define civilizations, however,

---

8 Samuel P Huntington, "The Clash of Civilisations", *Foreign Affairs* 72, 1993 No 3, 22-49. He developed his ideas in his book *The Clash of Civilisations and the Remaking of the World Order*, Simon and Schuster, Pbk. edtn, 1998, p.42.

the most important usually is religion, as the Athenians emphasized. To a very large degree, the major civilizations in human history have been closely identified with the world's great religions and people who share ethnicity and language but differ in religion may slaughter each other, as happened in Lebanon, the former Yugoslavia and in the Subcontinent.[9]

Huntington, who sees conflict as an inevitable feature of human behavior, predicted that the clash of civilizations, in which religion plays a major part, is likely to repeat itself, " ... as the world moves out of its Western phase".[10] In particular, Huntington foresaw a growing clash between the West and the civilization of Islam.

Huntington was right to highlight the link between religion and identity. Although Europe has had its share of religious wars, many people in the secularized West cannot understand the passion that religion can evoke and the bloody rivalry that it can cause. This is because religion has been pushed to the margins[11] and its role in the more traditional societies has been ignored.

Yet in affirming a person's identity and membership of a faith community, religion need not be divisive. This is the lesson we need to learn. The Native American spiritual leader Black Elk told of a dream in which he saw that the sacred hoop of his people was holy but also that it " ... was one of many hoops that made one circle, wide as daylight and as starlight".[12] Thankfulness for, and faithfulness to, our own faith tradition means we should understand the importance to other people of their faith tradition and learn to appreciate their inspiration and

---

9 *The Clash of Civilizations,* p.42.
10 *The Clash of Civilizations,* p.53-4.
11 In a report on a You Gov survey, Anthony King says "Most people give the impression of regarding religion as a consumer good, one to be consumed by those who happen to have a taste for it." *Daily Telegraph,* 27.12.04., p.16.
12 *1,000 World Prayers,* ed. Marcus Braybrooke, Omega Books, John Hunt Publishing, 2003, p.290.

beauty. Antagonism to others is often a sign of insecurity. As the British Chief Rabbi, Dr Jonathan Sacks has said, "The fact that the great universal monotheisms have not yet formally endorsed a plural world is still the unexercised darkness at the heart of our religious situation".[13]

I am not arguing for a monotonous monochrome society, where, for example, Christmas, Hanukah and Divali are merged into a hybrid "Winter Festival". At Madras Christian College, where I was a student, we had special meals to mark the festivals of each religion. The variety of celebrations can enrich a society. As the Queen said in her 2004 Christmas broadcast, "Diversity is a strength not a threat".[14]

Sadly, religious dogmas have made this recognition more difficult and indeed have often been a cause of prejudice - as for example, in the suffering caused to the Jewish people as a result of centuries of Christian anti-Jewish teaching. To speak well of another religion is sometimes heard as disloyalty to one's own faith. It is a commonplace among interfaith activists that as you make friends with people of other faiths, you make enemies in your own. At Madras Christian College, some of my Christian friends were perplexed when I wanted to visit Hindu temples. I understood that for some of their parents, conversion to Christianity had been very costly and had often meant ostracism from their family. But their attitude not only reflected the mentality of the missionary compound, but also the assumptions of religious and cultural superiority that accompanied imperialism.

A theology of the other

Talk of "the saved" or the "chosen people" or "the people of God", which is common in Christianity - and there are parallels in some other religions - has the negative implication that others are "unsaved", "unchosen" or "rejected by God". I have never liked the phrase

---

13 Jonathan Sacks, *The Persistence of Faith*, Weidenfeld and Nicolson, 1991, p.81.
14 *The Times*, 27.12.04., p.52.

"non-Christian", as you should not describe a person in negative terms: but I became more aware of this when I studied for a time in Israel and was conscious of being a "non-Jew".

Most Western societies encourage tolerance, although the relation of the state to faith communities varies from country to country and there are often limits to toleration. But tolerance is not enough. It allows others the right to be wrong, but does not remove the discriminatory influence of much traditional religious teaching. We need to see the positive contribution that another faith makes to human understanding of the Divine and the enrichment that it offers to one's own personal faith.[15] The Jewish scholar Shaye J D Cohen, has put this well when he wrote, "It is not enough simply to believe in tolerance, not enough simply to allow the other's existence, rather, what we need is a theology on each side to validate the other's existence".[16] Cohen challenged Jews to answer the question, "How is the divine cause somehow advanced by having millions and millions of Christians in the world?" He called on Christians to answer the question, "Why are the Jews still here?"[17] A similar challenge could well be applied to other religions as well.

In several religions there is a struggle between those who want to adopt a more open attitude and those who uphold traditional exclusive views.

In *Christian* circles, a rough distinction is often made between three approaches:

The exclusivist approach affirms that only through the atoning death of Jesus can people be restored to a right relation to God. Other religions do not offer salvation. This view means that only members of

---

15 I have tried to do this in my *What Can We Learn from Islam* and *What Can We Learn from Hinduism,* (both) John Hunt Publishing, 2002.
16 Shaye J D Cohen, "The Unfinished Agenda of Jewish-Christian Dialogue", *Journal of Ecumenical Studies,* Vol. 34, No 3, Summer 1997, p.326. See also my *Christian-Jewish Dialogue, The Next Steps,* SCM Press, 2000.
17 "The Unfinished Agenda", pp. 327-28.

the true church (usually taken to be the Roman Catholic Church) or those who have faith in Jesus Christ will be saved and go to heaven.

The inclusivist approach recognizes that God wants all people to be saved and that God's loving concern is for all people, but it also insists that God's final and full revelation is in Jesus Christ. Pope John Paul II, for example, said that "Although participated forms of mediation of different kinds and degrees are not excluded, they acquire meaning and value *only* from Christ's own mediation, and they cannot be understood as parallel or complementary to his".[18] Good people of other faiths may be saved by Christ even if they are not conscious of this and they are sometimes called "anonymous Christians". As Cardinal Arinze, who was President of the Pontifical Council for Inter-religious Dialogue, put it, "All human beings are included in the great and unique design of God in Jesus Christ, even when they are not aware of it".[19] Despite the intended generosity of this approach, it may seem condescending to members of other faiths, and it fails to give real value to the spiritual truths of other world religions.

The pluralist approach suggests that the mystery of God is indeed present in Jesus Christ, but also in other great spiritual figures such as the Buddha, or Rama or Krishna.[20] The individual believer can be loyal to a particular path without having to assert that his or her path is better than those followed by other believers.

There is an enormous literature on this subject and I have written about it elsewhere.[21] I gladly confess that it is through Jesus Christ that I have been met by God's love, but I do not see any need to sit in judgment on other people's spiritual experience. Instead I seek to learn from them more of the amazing grace of God. As Bishop George Appleton, a former Anglican Archbishop in Jerusalem and Editor of the

---

18 From the encyclical *Redemptoris Missio*, quoted by Fr. Thomas Ryan in his helpful article "Catholic Perspectives on Inter-religious Relations" in *Current Dialogue*, World Council of Churches, Geneva, No. 44, December 2004, p. 22

19 Cardinal Francis Arinze, "The Christian Commitment to Inter-religious Dialogue" in *L'Osservatore Romana*, 17.7.89, paragraphs 3 and 9.

20 This is far too brief a summary and there are several shades of opinion under each heading. See further Alan Race, *Christians and Religious Pluralism*, SCM Press 1983 and Revised edition, 1993, *passim*.

21 See my chapter in *Islam and Global Dialogue: Religious Pluralism and the Pursuit of Peace*, ed. Roger Boase, Ashgate, Aldershot, 2005.

Oxford Book of Prayer, wrote, "Each religion has a mission, a gospel, a central affirmation. Each of us needs to enlarge on the gospel, which he has received without wanting to demolish the gospel of others ... We can enlarge and deepen our initial and basic faith by the experience and insights of people from other religions and cultures, without disloyalty to our own commitment".[22]

The third option obviously facilitates interfaith co-operation, but to many Christians it seems to be a rejection of the traditional claim that Jesus Christ is the only Saviour and that Christianity is the only true religion. But there are several reasons why this traditional position should be questioned on both theological and philosophical grounds.[23]

First, the Biblical material is ambiguous. If some passages are exclusive, others are universalist and speak of God's concern for all people. Secondly, the Christian tradition is varied. For example, the second-century apologist Justin Martyr hoped to meet Plato in heaven and the great theologian St Thomas Aquinas held that it was possible for people who lived before Christ to be saved. So, thirdly, if God is the God of love whom Jesus proclaimed, then God's love is surely available to those who have not heard of Jesus. This suggests that other religions reveal at least something of God. Fourthly, as some Christians have got to know members of other faiths, they have recognized their genuine holiness. They have seen evidence of God's presence in other faith traditions. Fifthly, as Christians increasingly learn about other religions and read their Scriptures, they find them inspiring and genuine expressions of spirituality. Sixthly, critical study of the New Testament suggests that the focus of Jesus' message was on the kingdom of God rather than on his own status.[24] Seventhly, faith is primarily trust in the Living God not

---

22 George Appleton, "Faiths in Fellowship", *World Faiths*, No. 101, Spring 1977, pp.4-5.
23 There are many books on this subject. Wesley Ariarajah discusses the interpretation of the Bible in *The Bible and People of Other Faiths*, World Council of Churches, Geneva 1985. See also Jacques Dupuis, *Toward A Christian Theology of Religious Pluralism*, Orbis, Maryknoll, New York 1998, especially pp.29-52. He also gives a good summary of various Christian approaches to this subject. Michael Nazir-Ali's *Citizens and Exiles: Christian Faith in a Plural World*, SPCK 1998, gives a balanced summary of the issues, especially chapter 9. There are several books on the subject by Paul Knitter.
24 This is a summary of what I wrote in my *Time to Meet*, SCM Press, 1990. See pp. 84-92.

adherence to doctrines. Moreover, many Christians who are well versed in interfaith dialogue testify that it has both broadened and deepened their Christian faith.

Philosophically, the modern understanding of knowledge rejects "absolutism". It is recognized that all statements about reality – even in Holy Scripture - are conditioned by their author's historical setting, intention, culture, class and sex and that the same is true of the person who reads these statements. We are not in a position to make ultimate, unconditioned, statements. Even symbols, which are central to a religion, are not absolute and indeed are open to multiple interpretations.[25]

In *Judaism*, although God's covenant with Abraham[26] is central to Israel's self-understanding that they are a people chosen by God, several modern writers emphasize that this covenant was preceded by God's covenants with Adam[27] and with Noah,[28] which were covenants with *all* people. The choice of Israel was a special calling, but it does not exclude the possibility that God calls other nations to other tasks. Chief Rabbi Dr Sacks has written, "My own understanding of religious truth is that it is covenantal and that one covenant does not exclude another".[29]

Islam, which was often more tolerant of other faiths than mediaeval Christianity, recognizes Moses and Jesus as prophets. The Qur'an states that God sent a prophet to every people.[30] The message of these prophets was one and the same, but it is claimed that this message has been distorted by their followers. Only in the Qur'an is this message to be found in all its purity. So there is a universalism in Islam, especially in Sufism, although most Muslims claim that Islam is true and is the

---

25 See my *Faith and Interfaith in a Global Age,* CoNexus Press, Grand Rapids and Braybrooke Press, Oxford, 1998, Chapter 4 and 6.
26 Genesis 17.
27 Ecclesiasticus 17:11ff.
28 Genesis 9:9.
29 Sacks, p. 83 . He revised some parts of the first edition in response to criticism from some Ultra-Orthodox Jews.
30 Qur'an, 2,256.

standard by which other religious teaching is to be corrected.[31] God, however, it is said, chose to make more than one religion so that their followers would compete in good works.[32]

The religions of India have usually accepted that there are different paths to the Ultimate Mystery. Ancient Indian scriptures say, "Truth is one, sages call it by different names". *Hinduism* has in the last hundred years become known for its message of tolerance, although the reality in India is sometimes different. At the 1893 World Parliament of Religions, Swami Vivekananda declared, "We accept all religions as true".[33] Similarly, Mahatma Gandhi encouraged people to adhere firmly to their own religion and show equal reverence to other people's religions. He held that all religions lead to the same goal. *Sikhism* has also taught a message of tolerance. The founder, Guru Nanak said God's path "was neither Hindu nor Muslim".[34] The Dalai Lama, a *Buddhist*, is another great advocate of religious harmony. "My way to resolve the seeming contradiction between each religion's claim to 'one truth and one religion' and the reality of the multiplicity of faiths is to understand that in the case of a single individual, there can only be one truth, one religion. However, from the perspective of human society at large, we must accept the concept of 'many truths, many religions' … To my way of thinking, the diversity that exists amongst the various religious traditions is enormously enriching".[35]

Exclusive attitudes are changing, partly because the pioneers of the interfaith movement sensed that the Mystery of the Divine is greater than any one religious tradition's picture of the Divine. One pioneer was George Appleton, who said at the start of a service in which members

---

31 See my summary of Dr Zaki Badawi's Younghusband Lecture in *Pilgrimage of Hope*, SCM Press, 1992, p.78. I also summarised the lectures by Rabbi Dr Norman Solomon and Dr Robert Runcie. The full texts are available in the relevant copies of *World Faiths Insight*, June 1986, Feb 1986, and Oct 1986. See also Isma'il R Al Faruqi, Islam Argus Communications, Niles, Illinois, Chapter 1.
32 Qur'an, 5,48.
33 Swami Vivekananda in *The World's Parliament of Religions*, ed J H Barrows, The Parliament Publishing Co, Chicago, 1893, p.977.
34 Quoted by M P Fisher, *Living Religions*, Prentice Hall, 4th edtn. 1999, p 401.
35 HH the Dalai Lama, *Ancient Wisdom, Modern World*, Little Brown and Co, London 1999, p.235.

of several religions took part, "We stand in worship before the mystery of the final reality to whom or to which we give different names, so great and deep and eternal that we can never fully understand or grasp the mystery of His Being".[36] Another pioneer, the Indian philosopher Sarvepalli Radhakrishnan said, "The seers describe their experiences with an impressive unanimity. They are near to one another on mountains farthest apart".[37]

Ultimate Reality transcends any creedal definition or formula. Different religions express particular insights into the Divine mystery. Through mutual sharing, human appreciation of that Mystery may be enhanced. Difference is not to be feared but to be valued. Some religious leaders are threatened by this approach, which they label "indifferentism". They fear it may weaken members' loyalty to a particular faith. As a result, the relationship of the interfaith movement to the main line religions is still uneasy. At first most religious leaders opposed it, although a growing number now are supportive. Even so, Chief Rabbi Sacks, in his comments on the Millennium Summit of religious leaders at the UN in August 2000, found it easy to see "why religion is as often a cause of conflict as it is of conciliation … The peace spoken of was too often 'peace on our terms'".[38] Indeed at that Summit meeting, a Catholic cardinal and some Hindu swamis almost came to blows over the question of conversion.

Many leaders now support practical co-operation between faiths to promote peace and justice and to relieve human need, but still hold on to the view that theirs is the final or definitive revelation. This is not, I think, as John Hick has long argued, a tenable position. The

---

36 George Appleton was at one time Anglican Archbishop in Jerusalem and a Chair of the World Congress of Faiths. *World Faiths*, No 81, Autumn 1970, pp. 13-19, quoted in Marcus Braybrooke, *A Wider Vision*, Oneworld, 1996, pp.122-3.
37 S Radhakrishnan, "Fragments of a Confession" in *The Philosophy of Sarvepalli Radhakrishnan*, Ed. A Schlipp, Open Court, New York, 1952, p.62.
38 Jonathan Sacks, *The Dignity of Difference*, p.9.
39 The Press statement is published in *Current Dialogue*, World Council of Churches, Geneva, No 42, December 2003, p.35.

time has come for every religion to stop claiming that it is "the one and only" or the "best".[39] "We must welcome religious diversity and concede that no single religion can claim a monopoly of Truth ... Each faith has its contribution to make both separately and together".[40]

This is especially important when religions in many parts of the world are in danger of being hijacked by so called "fundamentalists" or extremists, some of whom misuse religion to spread hatred and violence.

"Fundamentalism"

Fundamentalism, strictly speaking, was a term first used at the end of the nineteenth century by Conservative Protestants, who affirmed that the Bible is literally inspired by God. The term now, rather confusingly, is applied to ultra-conservative members of other religions. It is misleading, however, to assume that because all Muslims accept the Qur'an as a direct revelation from God, they are necessarily fundamentalist in the pejorative sense that the word has acquired.

It is important to distinguish between traditionalists and fundamentalists. Traditionalists have not been challenged by many of the questions of modern society, whereas fundamentalists consciously reject many of the assumptions of modernism and post-modernism. Traditionalists have grown up in a religiously monochrome society and may never have questioned the truth of their religion.

In my childhood in Surrey, England, in the years after the Second World War, I was not really aware of religious options other than Christianity. Christianity provided the frame of reference for education and life and I was unaware that I saw life through Christian spectacles. Many other people have grown up with the unquestioned

---

40 "Welcome and Unwelcome Truths between Jews, Christians and Muslims: A Platform Statement from the Sternberg Centre JCM Dialogue Group", November 2004, printed in *Manna*, No. 86, Winter 2005, pp.2-3. See Appendix 1.

assumption that the religion of the society into which they were born is "true". They may have inherited that society's view that members of other religions were misguided, unenlightened, heathen or even destined to damnation. Only as you meet and have personal encounters with the "other" do you begin to question your traditional monolithic assumptions. This was illustrated to me by a friend whose daughter was very ill. At the weekend, a colleague at work who was a Hindu, rang her up to enquire after her child. "I have been praying for her," the colleague added. This, my friend told me, made her start questioning. "Who was the Hindu praying to?" "Was it another God or is there only one God whom Hindus and Christians address in different ways?" My friend had never thought about this before. She had not previously questioned the assumptions of the society in which she grew up.

Fundamentalists are aware of the questions raised by modern society, but turn their backs on them. Fundamentalists reassert traditional exclusive attitudes in defiance of the modern world. Fundamentalism is essentially oppositional and rejects new ways of thinking.[41] Fundamentalists vigorously oppose any change to their religious beliefs, although they may exploit modern means of communication. It is common place today to recognize that what we believe is partly the result of where and when we live. Although a clergyman of the Church of England, I do not share the outlook on the world of the sixteenth-century Archbishop Thomas Cranmer, who wrote the *Book of Common Prayer,* nor the mediaeval Christian preoccupation with the Last Judgment. Religious belief, in my view, like all knowledge is historically conditioned. Fundamentalists adopt an a-historical attitude to the central truths of their religion, which for them are unchanging and not open to reinterpretation in a changing world. They reject also the idea of symbolism, taking their particular myth as true in a literal sense. This also implies that other religions are false.[42] It

---

41 M E Marty, "What is Fundamentalism?" in *Fundamentalism as an Ecumenical Challenge,*Concilium Special, SCM Press, 1992.

is therefore a religious duty to oppose false teaching and also those who try to change traditional beliefs and practices.

Such opposition is even more the case when it is felt that the undermining of tradition is orchestrated by outsiders. The enormous economic and cultural impact of the West is associated in the minds of many Muslims and Hindus with Christianity because America and Western Europe are supposedly Christian countries. Western Europe is also remembered, especially in the Muslim world, as the agent of imperialism and the supporter of the "Zionist state". Israel is seen as an outpost of American imperialism. Thus, some extreme Muslims, for example members of Hamas, see military opposition to Israel, even suicide bombings, as a defense of their faith. Like some extreme Right Wing Jews, they use religious texts to reinforce claims to land and to justify the use of force.[43] American economic and military aggression against Iraq and some other Muslim countries is perceived by many Muslims as an attack on Islam.

Despite media coverage, it is very important to make clear, however, that Muslim fundamentalists speak only for a small minority of members of that faith. There is a real contemporary struggle for the soul of Islam. One Muslim said to me, "Instead of affirming that 'God is most great', fundamentalists are in effect saying that 'Islam is most great'".

Conclusion

It is not, however, only fundamentalists that exalt their religion rather than God. In the recent statement, from which I have already quoted of the Sternberg Centre's Jewish, Christian and Muslim Dialogue Group, of which I have been a member, acknowledges:

---

42 See further my article "Interfaith Can Save Religion for the World" in *Faith and Freedom,* Vol 52, no. 149, Autumn and Winter 1999, pp.125-133 and Leonard Swidler, *The Meaning of Life at the Edge of the Third Millennium,* Paulist Press, 1992.

43 Rabbi Henri Khan, an ultra-Orthodox leader in Israel has said, "Secular politicians have failed to grasp the religious significance for both sides in the current conflict (between Israel and Palestine). They are dealing with the situation as if it were purely a humanitarian issue whereas it is essentially an eschatological problem. There is a relationship between the text (scriptures) and what is happening today". Quoted by McTernan, p.118.

"In Jewish, Christian and Muslim and traditions one can find passages that have often been interpreted to support exclusive truth claims and a sense of superiority. In practice, each faith has been notably self-centered and lacking in self-criticism, claiming for itself a superior position and a unique authority."[44]

To repudiate such exclusivism would be a positive step that religions could make to reducing conflict in the world. It is even more urgent, as the Statement says, that "Scripture should not be used to justify violence, oppression, exploitation, military aggression or claims of superiority".[45]

---

44 "Welcome and Unwelcome Truths" *Manna*, p.2.
45 "Welcome and Unwelcome Truths" *Manna*, p.3.

ONLY NON-VIOLENCE
CAN BRING TRUE PEACE

ONLY NON-VIOLENCE CAN BRING TRUE PEACE

Religions have colluded with violence

Sadly, scriptures *have* often been used to justify violence and aggression. If people of faith are to be instruments of peace, they have first to acknowledge that religions have on many occasions embittered conflict and even sometimes have caused it. Until religions clean up their act, they lack credibility.

The use of violence, especially when it is given a religious justification, was ritually denounced by almost every speaker at the 2004 Parliament of World Religions, but it is too easy to say that claiming God's sanction for violence is just a misuse of religion. It is reckoned that religion is a contributory cause in more than half of the 115 armed conflicts which occurred between 1989 and 2001.[1] With some justice, it has been said, "the daily news seems a catalogue of holy hatred".[2]

How much should religion be blamed for violence? This is a hotly disputed question. Some people, such as Mikhail Bakuin, a nineteenth-century Russian scholar, put almost all the blame on religion. Bakuin argued that there is an indissoluble link between religion and sacrifice and as such "all religions are cruel, all founded on blood; for all rest principally on the idea of sacrifice".[3] A more common

1 Oliver McTernan, *Violence in God's Name*, Orbis, 2003, p.xiii
2 James a Haught, *Holy Hatred: Religious Conflicts of the '90s*, Prometheus Books, Amherst NY, 1995, quoted in the Parliament of Religions preparatory paper "Overcoming Religiously Motivated Violence", p.69. No page reference is given.
3 Mikhail Bakuin, "God and the State" in *Selected Writings*, ed. A Lehning, Grove Press, New York, 1974, 111-35, p.126. See also Rene Girard, *Violence and the Sacred*, ET Patrick Gregory, The John Hopkins University Press, Baltimore. The original French version was published in 1972; and D L Coppola, "The Problem of Religion, Violence and Peace: An Uneasy Trilogy" in *Religion and Violence: Religion and Peace*, ed J H Ehrenkranz and D L Coppola, Sacred Heart University Press, Fairfield, Connecticut, 2000.

charge against religions, as Huntington argues, is that they reinforce national and ethnic divisions and that they have too often endorsed the use of violence.[4] The basic causes of violence, however, are more often social, political or economic. Religious difference then embitters the ensuing conflict. The Carnegie Commission, rightly in my view, argued that "religious diversity does not spawn violence independently of predisposing social, economic and political conditions as well as the subjective roles of belligerent leaders".[5] Paul Collier of the World Bank also claims that the most likely cause of conflict and civil strife is economic greed and the hope of getting rich by seizing control of valuable assets.[6] Ted Gurr, Director of a Minority at Risk program, argues however that "discrimination and repression and resentment provide strong incentives for … protest and rebellion".[7]

The causes of conflict are clearly complex and varied. Yet, even if religion is not the basic cause of violence, the way in which some people expect God to bless acts of terror is chilling. A document found in the luggage of one of the Nine-Eleven hijackers is terrifying evidence of the way religion can be twisted to sanction killing. The letter, by Mohammed Atta, told his fellow conspirators to shave excess hair from the body, to shower, to wear cologne, to rehearse their plan of action, and to read and reflect on the war texts of the Qur'an:

> Tame your soul, purify it, convince it, make it
> understand, and incite it … Bless your body with
> some verses of the Qur'an – this is done by
> reading verses into one's hands and then rubbing
> the hands over whatever is to be blessed – the

---

4 See further, Karen Armstrong, *Holy War,* Macmillan, 1988.
5 The Carnegie Commission on Preventing Deadly Conflict, 1997, *Preventing Deadly Conflict: Final Report,* Washington, DC, p. 29. Bruce Lincoln, a historian of religion, reached the same conclusion. He wrote that in most of the post Cold War conflicts in which religious issues have played a role, it was "in contexts where structural problems inherent to the nation-state have become manifest: specifically the potential contradiction between nation and state". Bruce Lincoln, "Conflict" in *Critical Terms for Religious Studies,* ed. Mark C Taylor, University of Chicago Press, 1998, pp. 57- 8.
6 Paul Collier and Anke Hoeffler, *Greed and Grievance in Civil War,* A World Bank Report, 2001. Quoted by Oliver McTernan, p.10.
7 Ted Robert Gurr, "Peoples Against States: Ethno Political Conflict and the Changing World System", *International Studies Quarterly* (1994), 38, pp. 347-77, quoted by Oliver McTernan, p.15.

luggage, the clothes, the knife, your personal
effects, your ID, your passport … the rest is left
to God, the best one to depend on … We will all
meet in the highest heaven, God willing.[8]

But don't let me single out Islam! My wife, Mary, and I were in
Israel on the day when Prime Minister Yitzhak Rabin was assassinated.
Yigal Amir, the pious and articulate Jewish university student who was
arrested after the attack, was said to have had no regrets, believing that
he acted "on orders from God". He claimed later that some militant
rabbis had said that the killing of the Prime Minister would be justified
because he was putting the security of the Jewish people at risk.[9]
Christian paramilitary groups in Indonesia claim that their use of
violence against Muslims is in defense of Christianity. The bloodstained
Serb leader Radovan Karadzic was decorated by the Greek Orthodox
Church as "one of the most prominent sons of our Lord Jesus Christ
working for peace".[10]

These are extreme examples, but most religions have been
ambiguous in their attitude to the use of force. They have extolled the
virtue of peace, but thought of this as a relationship with ultimate
reality, not as a goal to be achieved in this world. Religious leaders in
many societies have been constrained in their opposition to the warlike
policies of governments because they wished to protect their privileged
position and the property of their faith community. Above all, as
William Frost says at the end of his nearly nine hundred-page study of
religious perspectives on war and peace, "religious institutions do not
make peace their primary value, because their sacred scriptures accept
and even exalt war. The sacred books of religions, even while they
proclaim the ultimate value of peace also portray violence in a favorable

---

8 From *The New York Times*, 29.11.01, quoted by Oliver McTernan, p.22
9 From *The New York Time*, 5.11.95, quoted by Oliver McTernan, p.31.
10 Oliver McTernan, pp.30-31.

light ... When religion teaches peace, it also validates war".[11] Indeed, God is portrayed as a God of War, not only in the first chapters of the Bible, but in other scriptures. This emphasizes the need for a critical reading of scripture and the dangers of the fundamentalists' use of proof texts.

Religions in their teachings have tried to limit the suffering and damage that is caused by war. Tragically, they have seldom clearly proclaimed the way of non-violence to be found in the preaching of Jesus and the Buddha. We need today to hear again that message in all its original clarity – a message that reflects the fundamental spiritual insight that every life is precious to God.

The teaching of religions on the use of force

Although the early *Christians* were pacifist, when the Roman Empire adopted Christianity, the Church gradually developed the doctrine of the just war. Augustine helped to shape this teaching, but the first systematic account appeared in the *Decretum* of Gratian, who died in the middle of the twelfth century. According to this theory, a war can be thought just if, first, it is undertaken to regain something that was wrongfully taken or to punish evil or in defense against planned or actual aggression. Secondly, the war has to be initiated by legitimate authority. Thirdly, a right intention on the part of those involved is required. Fourthly, the use of force must be proportional, that is to say relevant to the issue and not do more harm than good.[12] Traditionally, a just war had to be for the sake of peace and have a reasonable hope of success. The teaching also tried to limit the cruelties of war. Although the majority of Christians have accepted that force may be necessary to

---

11 J.William Frost, *A History of Christian, Jewish, Hindu, Buddhist and Muslim Perspectives on War and Peace*, The Edwin Mellen Press, Lewiston, New York, 2004. Vol. II, p.779.
12 The excessive so-called "co-lateral" damage in recent campaigns in Kosovo and Iraq would make these wars unjust on this count alone. It is reckoned that nearly 100,000 people have died in the war in Iraq.

check violence and oppression, there have always been Peace Churches, such as the Mennonites and the Society of Friends. More recently a number of Christians, who are not pacifist *per se*, have argued that nuclear weapons were bound to do more harm than good.

The teachings of the Qur'an and of *Muslim* jurists are similar. Traditional Muslim teaching insists that the use of force is only allowed in certain clearly defined situations of self-defense or to protect innocent victims. Efforts were made to limit the cruelties of war. Islamic teaching normally only allows war under three conditions. First, force can be used to oppose and expel those who attack Muslims without just cause. Secondly, it is permissible to prevent oppression and persecution of the faithful. This provision may be extended to the protection of those who are not Muslim but who are victims of unjustified aggression. Thirdly, force could be used to protect places intended for the worship of God – not only mosques, but also churches and synagogues.

The Qur'an describes war as a conflagration. God's aim is to put it out. "Every time they kindle the fire of war, Allah doth extinguish it".[13] The Qur'an tries to limit the evils of war. Should the enemy desist from fighting, Muslims should do the same, because "Allah is Oft-Forgiving, Most Merciful".[14] Cruelty such as disfiguring the enemy dead or torturing prisoners is forbidden. Plundering was forbidden and also unnecessary damage such as cutting down fruit trees.

Even so, the use of force, in some circumstances, is justified in Islam. It is in this context that the word *jihad* is to be understood. *Jihad* is often taken to mean "religious" war, but that is misleading. The word *jihad* means striving, especially striving in the cause of God. The Sufi mystics emphasize that the purifying of the inner self is more important than physical struggle against the enemies of Islam.[15] A Muslim is expected to promote the message of Islam through his words and

13 Qur'an, 5, 64.
14 Qur'an, 2, 191.
15 See further my *What Can We Learn from Islam*, John Hunt Publishing, 2002, p.85.

actions. The Qur'an makes clear that "there can be no compulsion in religion: Truth stands out clear from Error".[16] Non-believers who were willing to submit, should be accepted and there was special provision for Christians and Jews – "People of the Book" *Jihad* does not imply the killing of non-believers just because of their lack of faith. *Jihad* is in defense of Islam and the vulnerable. *Jihad* is not regarded as one of the pillars of Islam.

Traditionally *Judaism* has stressed the blessings of peace. After the Second World War and the horrors of the Holocaust, however, Jews in Israel fought vigorously for the survival of the new state. More recently the Israeli army invaded Lebanon, and in its struggle against "terrorism", it has been very oppressive of Palestinians in Gaza and the West Bank. Such policies have been criticized by Jewish human rights groups and some religious groups both in Israel and in the Diaspora.

Although there are some Jewish pacifists,[17] Rabbi Dr Louis Jacob is right to say that "although Judaism sets the highest store on peace, it does not adopt a completely pacifist stand … Judaism treats warfare as a necessary evil but an evil nonetheless".[18]

Hinduism today is associated in many people's minds with Gandhi's teaching of *ahimsa* or non-violence. *Ahimsa* is an ancient concept, but the great Hindu epics, the Mahabharata and the Ramayana, are stories of war and conquest, although they do not disguise the suffering and destruction caused by war. In the *Bhagavad Gita*, Arjuna is told to go into battle to uphold *dharma* (religious duty), even if it means killing his own relatives. Violence is not wrong in self-defense nor in upholding the divinely constituted order of society. The concept of a just and righteous war also appears in the Arthashastra.[19]

16 The Qur'an, 2, 256.
17 See *The Challenge of Shalom: The Jewish Tradition of Peace and Justice,* Ed. Murray Polner and Naomi Goodman, New Society Publishers, Philadelphia, 1994.
18 Louis Jacobs, *Concise Companion to the Jewish Religion,* Oxford University Press, 1999, p 292.
19 Werner Menski in *Ethical Issues in Six Religious Traditions,* Ed Peggy Morgan and Clive Lawton, Edinburgh University Press, 1996, pp.44-47 . See also Henry O Thompson, *World Religions in War and Peace,* McFarland and Co, Jefferson, North Carolina, 1988 and John Ferguson, *War and Peace in the World's Religions,* 1978.

The first precept in *Buddhism* is to refrain from harming any living being, so Buddhism clearly opposes violence. It teaches that "Hatred is never appeased by hatred in this world; it is appeased by love". If it is necessary to kill someone to protect the innocent, then in Theravada Buddhism this will produce serious karmic consequences, even if the intention is recognized. In Mahayana Buddhism, if the action is done with complete unselfishness and for the sake of other sentient beings, it is not wrong and may not produce bad *karma*. Of course, not all Buddhists have lived up to the teaching, and Buddhist countries have not been free from conflict, although perhaps there has been less glorification of war.[20]

It is clear that most religions have failed unequivocally to condemn violence and killing. Because of this, terrorists can distort religious teaching and find verses in scripture – quoted uncritically and out of context - to justify their actions. It is time to reject the just war theory and its variants and to insist that violence, even if it is a short-term solution, is never the answer and breeds future violence.[21]

In 1983, I was at a small meeting in preparation for the World Council of Churches Assembly at Vancouver. The group suggested that the Assembly should call on all religions to cease justifying war – or to "de-legitimize war". Nothing came of this. But such a move has become ever more urgent. The problems of how to deal with tyrannical rulers and with those who perpetrate genocide and acts of terrorism are real enough, but the deep wisdom of the sacred scriptures is that violence begets violence. It is time for religions to help reverse the escalating

---

20 Peggy Morgan in *Ethical Issues in Six Religious Traditions*, pp.88-90.
21 Oliver McTernan summarises his historical overview of the teaching of the main religions in this way: "Without exception each faith community has, in the face of the threat of extinction or the opportunity to expand, interpreted its fundamental teaching to accommodate the changing circumstances by sanctioning the use of violence to protect and secure its own sectarian interests. In each faith tradition one can find sufficient ambiguity in its founding texts and stories to justify killing for the glory of God. Each tradition has also its heroes who saw themselves acting on divine authority as they plotted the destruction of those whom they perceived to be enemies of God. Today's religious extremists can find their rationale for inflicting terror in the name of their God in the ambivalence towards violence that is to be found in each faith tradition." *Violence in God's Name*, p.76.

violence in the world by listening again to the teaching of Jesus and the Buddha and unambiguously affirming that only through non-violent means can lasting peace and justice be secured.

The call for non-violence

"Love your enemies, do good to those who hate you".[22] These words of Jesus were part of the gospel reading at a service in Assisi which my wife and I attended as I started to revise this chapter. We were in the Lower Church of the Basilica de San Francesca, just above the tomb of St Francis, who perhaps more than any of Jesus' followers took his Lord's words literally. When Francis made his way to Syria, where the "Christian" crusaders were besieging Damietta, he was sickened by the brutality. Convinced that the gospel of love could not be imposed by the sword, Francis walked across no-man's land. He was taken into the presence of the Sultan, who was astonished by his words of peace.

Christians may hope to be forgiven for not living up to the teaching of Jesus: but they may well not be forgiven for diluting that teaching. Christians need to proclaim the unambiguous message of Jesus, which he reiterated. "You must love your enemies and do good to them".[23]

Although, as we have seen, many Christians have accepted the just war theory, it has no basis in the teaching and example of Jesus. The Buddha also taught that, "In those who harbor such thoughts as 'he abused me, he struck me, he overcame me, he robbed me' – hatred never ceases. In those who do not harbor such thoughts, hatred will cease. Hatred never ceases by hatred in this world; through non-enmity it comes to an end. This is an ancient law".[24] The Buddha taught, "Do not kill a living being. You should not kill or condone killing by others.

---

22 Luke 6:27.
23 Luke 6:35.
24 *Dhammapada 13-6*, quoted by Ferguson, p.49.
25 Suttanipata 394, see Ferguson, p.47.

You should abandon the use of violence. You should not use force either against the strong or against the weak".[25]

Jesus and the Buddha did not have the responsibility of governing. Muhammad, as a ruler, had to wrestle with the use of power. Muhammad had responded patiently to the hostility and ridicule he met with in Mecca during the early years of his ministry. In 622 CE, he was invited to become leader and ruler of the neighboring town of Madina. From there, in due course, he led an attack on Mecca and captured it. There are various economic, social and political factors that contributed to the Prophet's victory and to subsequent Muslim expansion. The point is that Muhammad accepted the necessity of the use of force. The command of God had been "Recite". "Your only duty is to deliver (the message)", God told the prophet.[26] Yet his preaching met with a meager response. Is it sufficient to proclaim God's message and accept its rejection or should a person use the means available to them to ensure its success – even, in the last resort, to the use of violence? Ibn Khaldun (1332-1402), a distinguished historian and philosopher, who has been called the father of sociology, said that verbal propagation of a faith is incomplete. He did not consider Christianity to be a missionary religion precisely because it had no *jihad*. The contemporary Muslim writer Fazlur Rahman has also said, "It is part of the Qur'anic doctrine that simply to deliver the message, to suffer frustration, and not to succeed, is immature spirituality".[27]

The comparison of the choice made by Muhammad and Jesus has clarified my own thinking and made me more aware of the challenge of the Cross. It has deepened my commitment to the way of non-violent suffering love. But I am aware of the painful choices this also entails. Does it make one appear to stand aside in the face of evil and terrible suffering?[28] This would be the criticism of many Muslims

---

26 Qur'an 42, 48.
27 Fazlur Rahman, *Islam*, London 1961, p.15.
28 I explore this question more fully in *What Can We Learn from Islam?*

and indeed of some Christians, but non-violence has to be combined with an active struggle against oppression and evil.

Jesus himself did not opt out of the struggle for justice. He challenged the prejudices of his day and was willing to die for his convictions. In recent times, it is Gandhi and Martin Luther King, who have most clearly taught and used non-violent protest to effect social change. Gandhi's emphasis was on the positive power of sacrificial selfless love, rather than on non-violence. He combined the idea of *ahimsa*, which he learned from the Jains of his native Gujarat and the sense of duty for duty's sake,[29] which is taught in the *Bhagavad Gita*. He was also inspired by Jesus' Sermon on the Mount and by the writings of Thoreau, Ruskin and Tolstoy. Gandhi's chosen term was *Satyagraha* - the force of truth – because it had a positive meaning, whereas to him, pacifism was a negative term describing a negative response to oppression. Pacifism was also an English word![30] "Truth (*satya*)," he said, "implies love, and firmness (*agraha)* engenders and therefore serves as a synonym for force. I thus began to call the Indian movement 'Satyagraha', that is to say, Force which is born of Truth and Love or non-violence, and gave up the use of the phrase 'passive resistance'".

Satyagraha involves the acceptance of suffering for oneself and the desire to do good to one's adversary. "*Satyagraha* postulates the conquest of the adversary by suffering in one's own person".[31] Gandhi's aim was not to defeat the opponent but to appeal to his or her higher nature.

Martin Luther King was also clear that non-violent resistance was not for cowards. Its aim was "not to defeat or humiliate the opponent, but to win his friendship and understanding".[32] At the end of a non-violent campaign, Martin Luther King hoped there would be greater understanding and even respect between those who opposed

---

29 *nishkarma karma.*
30 See Peter D Bishop, *A Technique for Loving,* SCM Press 1981, p.51ff and p.83.
31 *The Selected Writings of Mahatma Gandhi,* Vol. III, Ahmedabad, 1968, 157.
32 Martin Luther King, *Stride Toward Freedom,* Gollancz, 1959, p.96.

each other instead of the bitterness and resentment which those who have been defeated usually feel. His campaign, he insisted was against the "forces of evil rather than against persons who happen to be doing evil … We are out to defeat injustice and not white persons who may be unjust".[33] Like Gandhi, Martin Luther King also accepted the possibility of suffering, believing as the New Testament taught, that suffering love could be redemptive. Moreover, he was convinced that "the universe is on the side of justice". The non-violent resister "knows that in his struggle for justice he has cosmic companionship".[34]

People often challenge those who advocate non-violence by asking what they would do if they saw an armed man killing a group of innocent children. Would they themselves use firearms if they were available? Advocates of non-violence are not so naïve that they think the world can be changed overnight. What is needed is to create a culture of peace. Steps can also be taken to reduce the level of violence. The use of armed force should come under the control of international peacekeeping authorities. Gandhi admitted, "I have to concede that even in a non-violent state a police force may be necessary".[35] UN peacekeeping forces can have a similar role and act as an international police force, but this means that the UN has to become a more effective body and member states surrender more of their sovereignty to it.

The Dalai Lama, believing that violence begets violence and inevitably causes suffering, argues for a whole new mind-set that sees war for what it really is, that is a "fire" that spreads and whose fuel is living people. Emphasizing the need for everyone to create the external conditions for disarmament by inner purification and by countering their negative thoughts and emotions, he recognizes that "military dis-establishment" cannot be achieved overnight. But he insists the world

---

33 *Stride Toward Freedom*, p.96.
34 *Stride Toward Freedom*, p.100.
35 *Harijan*, 1.9.1940.

cannot hope to enjoy true peace as long as authoritarian regimes are propped up by armed force. A global police force is necessary, which "would protect against the appropriation of power by violent means".[36]

It is a massive task to create a culture of peace, but if religions do not take the lead, no one else will. I pray that religious leaders will live up to the commitment they made at the Millennium World Peace Summit, "to manage and resolve non-violently the conflicts generated by religious and ethnic differences, and to condemn all violence committed in the name of religion while seeking to remove the roots of the violence".[37]

---

[36] HH The Dalai Lama, *Ethics for the New Millennium,* Riverhead Books, New York, 1999, p.207 and p.212
[37] "Commitment to Global Peace", A Statement of the Millennium World Peace Summit of Religions and Spiritual Leaders, held at the UN in New York in August 2000.

A CULTURE OF PEACE

A Culture of Peace

At its heart, a culture of peace requires an inner transformation so that we recognize the sacredness of the other. The Mayan spiritual leader, Abraham Garcia, who was tortured in the civil war in Guatemala, has said, "Peace isn't the simple silencing of the bullets. It must be an inner change toward other people, respect for the way they think and live".[1] Peace education at every stage in life, from the earliest years in the home, is vital, and faiths need to continue to give priority to spiritual formation.

There are, however, more specific measures they can take to create a more peaceful world. Religious communities, as I have argued in the first chapter, should give a lead by ridding themselves of the suspicion, hostility and competitiveness they have so often shown to each other. Secondly they must preach a message of human unity, challenge false nationalism and encourage support for international law and international agencies. Thirdly, they need to champion the poor, oppose the arms trade and seek a new world order based on a shared ethic. They also need to engage even more strongly in practical peace building efforts.

What can people of faith do to reduce conflict?

The above still sounds rather general. Here are some suggestions and examples of how faith communities can work together to give practical

---

1 Quoted in Marcus Braybrooke, *365 Meditations for a Peaceful Heart and a Peaceful World*, Godsfield Books, 2004, p.296.

effect to such good intentions, although I recognize faith communities are not united and there are strong conservative elements in some religions which oppose interfaith co-operation and the agenda I am suggesting.

People of faith working together could have a major preventative role in helping to remove causes of conflict. They could also make a valuable contribution to peace building after conflict. I am less confident about what can be achieved during a conflict. I shall try to look at these three scenarios, aware of the varying local, national and international levels.

Preventative work

Faith communities, as we have seen, have often been competitive and suspicious of, or hostile to, other faith communities – both of the same religion or of another religion. The last hundred years have seen strenuous efforts to reverse this traditional antagonism. Over the last hundred years interfaith groups have done significant work in transforming the attitude of members of one faith community to members of other faiths, but this work has been of only limited success, partly because of lack of resources and partly because many people are not very interested in their own religion, let alone other people's religions. Moreover, prejudice, like the weeds in a garden, reappear as soon as one's back is turned. Constant vigilance is necessary because prejudice in all its forms is "a very light sleeper".[2]

An example of progress: Christians and Jews

For change to happen, people must be convinced it is possible. The dramatic change in Christian-Jewish relations in the last fifty years is an

---

2 The Runnyemede Trust produced a report called "Anti-Semitism is a Very Light Sleeper".

example that old hostilities can be overcome. Indeed, Gerald Priestland, a distinguished BBC Religious Affairs correspondent, said that the new relationship between Jews and Christians in Britain was one of the very few items of genuinely good news on which he was able to report.

The shock and horror of the Holocaust has made Christians increasingly aware that it was the anti-Jewish preaching of the Church that prepared a seed bed in the heart of Christendom in which the deadly weed of Nazism could grow. The Nazis were anti-Christian as well as anti-Jewish, but they exploited the Church's traditional teaching of contempt. The task of building a new understanding and relationship has required Christians to correct their picture of Judaism in the first century, and especially the role of the Pharisees. It is now widely recognized that Jesus was a faithful Jew and that Judaism has continued as a spiritually creative religion. Whereas Christians used to think that God had broken off the covenant with Israel and banished Jews from the Holy Land because of the death of Jesus, most churches now recognize that the covenant with the Jewish people is still valid. This has led many Christians to reject missionary attempts to convert Jews. Moreover, some Christians have openly confessed the injury done to the Jewish people and have asked forgiveness, as Pope John Paul II did in Jerusalem in May 2000.[3]

Certain stages in the new relationship between Jews and Christians can be identified. The first has been to dispel ignorance and prejudice. In part this was the result of work by both Jewish and Christian scholars to correct past misinformation and to embark on a major effort to educate members of both communities in the new knowledge. Equally important was the personal meeting and growing friendship of ordinary Christians and Jews encouraged by Councils of Christians and Jews in many countries. On the Christian side, as already indicated, the new appreciation of Judaism has led to theological

---

3 See further my, *Time to Meet*, SCM Press, 1990 and *Christian-Jewish Dialogue: The Next Steps*, SCM Press, 2000.

rethinking. As Christians and Jews have overcome past prejudices, they have increasingly affirmed what they have in common, especially in the areas of ethical and moral teachings and have begun to witness together to these values in the wider society.

In the churches' relationship to other religions there has not been the motivation of the horrors of the Holocaust, but in relation to Islam, crusades and imperialism have left a dangerous legacy. There is an enormous task to correct ignorance and prejudice, particularly Islamophobia, which is fed by ignorant and biased material in much of the media.[4] The Muslim community, in Britain and in several other countries, is now seeking dialogue with Christians and Jews – as for example in the Three Faiths Forum. Instead of past denunciations, some Christians now appreciate the spiritual profundity of Islam and I agree with Christian thinkers who recognize that Muhammad was a true prophet of God, even if not, for Christians, the final prophet.[5] In a similar way some Christians, such as Fr. Bede Griffiths, who was the guru of a Christian ashram in Southern India, have learned to recognize the deep spiritual wisdom of India. Across the world, crowds flock to hear the Dalai Lama.[6]

There has, as far as I know, been little attempt of Hindu, Muslim and Sikh scholars to look together at their often tragic histories, although at several Sikh conferences which I have attended in the Punjab, Hindu and Muslim speakers are also regularly invited to participate.

The growth of the study of religions has provided better information about the religions of the world and encouraged fruitful collaboration. Although this is mainly in the realm of academia, its influence has spread in some countries to schools and to the more general public through the many books now available about the

---

4 See *Islamaphobia – a Challenge for Us All*, The Runnymede Trust, 1997.
5 See my *What Can We Learn from Islam*, John Hunt Publishing, 2002, pp.42ff.
6 See my *What Can We Learn from Hinduism*, John Hunt Publishing 2002, *passim*.

religions of the world and through documentary programs on television.

Education can play a vital part in creating a sympathetic appreciation of the other. A project was initiated with some support from Israeli and Palestinian authorities called "Teaching About the Other" to see how Israeli and Palestinian children could be given a sympathetic view of each other's religion and a reasonably objective history of the conflict in the twentieth century.[7] Similar projects have been undertaken in Northern Ireland.

The provision for teaching religion in schools varies from country to country. It is alarming that this is seldom adequately resourced when we consider the dangers of false information and prejudice. Faith communities also have done too little to ensure that what their members say and write about members of other faiths encourages respect rather than hostility. Although there has been a steady increase in many countries of local interfaith groups, far more also needs to be done to support the work of local interfaith councils and to encourage members of faith communities to get to know each other. Visits to synagogues, mosques, temples and *gurdwaras* are a good way, as are shared meals. At the Barcelona Parliament of Religions, a great sense of fellowship was created by the Sikhs, who arranged a great *langar,* or community kitchen, in a marquee on the seashore where anyone could come for a free lunch.

Faith communities also have a responsibility to challenge prejudicial remarks made in the media, not only about themselves but about other faith communities. The Three Faiths Forum – of Jews, Christians and Muslims - has been particularly effective in such work. It has issued statements condemning all forms of violence in the Middle East and in the Balkans and denouncing acts of terror.

---

7 The research was being undertaken by Dr Coos Schoneveld.

Symbolism

After the September 11th attack on the twin towers, members of many faiths came together across the USA to express their sympathy and solidarity. Such symbolic occasions are of great importance. The relation of the state to religion differs from country to country. In England, the Church of England is the Established Church and civic religious occasions were until about twenty years ago mostly Anglican, with sometimes token participation of Roman Catholics and members of the Free Churches. In the 'seventies, to the anger of some Christians, the Commonwealth Day Observation, which the Queen usually attends, set a precedent by including Hindu, Buddhist, Muslim and Sikh readings. For a time the observance was held at the Guildhall - a religiously neutral venue. For many years, however, it has been held in Westminster Abbey. Now it is much more common for members of the main faiths in Britain to take part in any civic service. If a service is held to mark the inauguration of a new mayor, it may be held in a Sikh *gurdwara*, a Hindu temple or a mosque. In South Africa, with the end of *apartheid*, the first parliament was inaugurated with prayers from several religions.

Symbolism is significant in helping to develop the public's mind-set. The image conveyed by the media of the situation in Northern Ireland is one of religious conflict. Even there, however, a small interfaith group is acting as a leaven to transform society. In Belfast, the Interfaith Forum has provided a beautiful meditation room for people of all faiths. The Interfaith Forum is also lobbying the government to include the teaching of all world religions in the school curriculum.

Buildings themselves can be symbolic. St Ethelburga Church in the City of London, which was ruined by a terrorist bomb, now houses the St Ethelburga Centre for Reconciliation and Peace. Two other churches, Coventry Cathedral and the Frauenkirche in Dresden, which were destroyed by the blanket bombing of their cities during World War

II, have also become centers of work for reconciliation and symbols of the power of faith to turn enmity into friendship. Among the memorials in the Peace Memorial Park in Hiroshima is a Peace Cairn, next to the Children's Peace Monument, which is built of stone quarried from the Scottish mountain of Ben Nevis. It was given by young people from Fort William in Scotland and Dudley in England "as a symbol of goodwill and desire for reconciliation and world peace".[8]

A voice of protest

Religions also have an important role in shaping public opinion. The poet W H Auden said, "All I have is a voice to undo the folded lie",[9] but the voice of protest can be very powerful, as we have seen most recently in the Ukraine. The voice of millions raised in protest also helped to topple Communist regimes in Eastern Europe. In Poland especially and in East Germany, the churches were a focus for the opposition to Communist governments. Many people of faith and good will do speak out against the abuse of human rights, the spiraling arms trade and the widespread use of torture – to mention just a few prevalent abuses – but the voice needs to be stronger and more insistent. The power of prayer, fostered by the Week of Prayer for World Peace, the Peace Prayer Movement and other groups, should not be underestimated. The mid eighties saw a wave of prayer for peace, including the Million Minutes for Peace Campaign and the World Day of Prayer for Peace, convened by the Pope, at Assisi in 1986, - held before Presidents Gorbachov and Reagan had met for the first time.

The impact of faith communities would be greater if they spoke with a more united voice and were more willing to join together in prayer for peace. The Peace Council, whose members include the

---

8 Yoshiteru Kosakai, *Hiroshima Peace Reader,* Hiroshima Peace Culture Foundation, 1980, p.62.
9 W H Auden's poem "September 1st, 1939' was published in 1940. It includes the line, 'We must love one another or die".

Dalai Lama, Ma Goshananda, the senior Cambodian Buddhist monk and Archbishop Desmond Tutu, spoke out against the use of land mines, and the Council, during the conferences which led to the treaty to ban Landmines, arranged a series of interfaith prayer services. The longer established World Conference on Religion and Peace initially brought to bear the voice of religions against the dangers of nuclear warfare. Recently it has given much attention to conflict resolution and has been particularly active in Sierra Leone and in the Balkans.

Religions still have considerable moral authority and can activate world opinion because of their involvement in local communities across the world. It is a dangerous temptation to assume power rests with politicians, armies and militias. I once heard President Gorbachov say that change begins with a few people who have a vision. Gradually they gather support. With enough support they attract the attention of the media and then politicians begin to listen and – often grudgingly – begin to act. Desmond Tutu, who in the new South Africa has worked for reconciliation, spoke out courageously against *apartheid.*

Many people wish the voice of religions was more audible and effective in the modern world. At the Day of Prayer in Assisi, the Pope told his fellow leaders, "We are the moral conscience of human kind". It is a conscience that needs to speak more loudly and with greater authority. This is why many people would like to see a Religious or Spiritual Council to voice shared concerns and to advise and support the United Nations. Indeed, even before the United Nations was formed, Bishop Bell of Chichester suggested in the House of Lords in 1943 that an Advisory Committee with representatives of all the major faiths should be formed to work with the UN. The World Congress of Faiths gained some support for this but by the time the first meeting of the UN was held in London, the Iron Curtain had divided the world into two power blocks. Communist states were hostile to all religions and prevented the UN from engaging with religious leaders. It was not until the collapse of Communism that new possibilities opened up to exert some influence on the UN. Yet even now, despite various suggestions, there is no Spiritual Advisory Council nor World Religions Council at the UN.

The positive contribution of religions to a new world order

Much interfaith work to reduce conflict already described is essentially reactive. Can religions also be proactive and help to create a more just and peaceful world order? This is an urgent challenge. At the 1993 Parliament of Religions in Chicago, as we have seen, most members of the Assembly signed a document called "Toward a Global Ethic".[10] Subsequently, as already mentioned, the Council for a Parliament of the World's Religions has attempted to show how these ethical demands can affect the life of our society. Prior to the 1999 Cape Town Parliament of Religions "A Call to our Guiding Institutions" was issued inviting leaders of government, business, education, arts and media, science and medicine, intergovernmental organizations and the organizations of civil society, as well as those in positions of religious and spiritual leadership to "build new, reliable, and more imaginative partnerships towards the shaping of a better world".[11]

The Call was issued at an opportune moment. As the focus of much interfaith activity has become more practical, many people who are in positions of leadership in the political and economic spheres are both recognizing the importance of religion in shaping the modern world and acknowledging that there is a spiritual and ethical dimension to the major problems facing humankind. There is space only to give a few examples of this development.

Since 1993, UNESCO has held several conferences addressing

---

10 *A Global Ethic: A Declaration of the Parliament of the World's Religions,* Ed Hans Kung and Karl-Josef Kuschel, SCM Press 1993. See below p. 89
11 "A Call to Our Guiding Institutions", Council for a Parliament of the World's Religions, Chicago 1999.

the role of religion in conflict situations and at the 1994 conference in Barcelona issued a "Declaration on the Role of Religion in the Promotion of a Culture of Peace". UNESCO has established an International Inter-religious Advisory Committee and with the UN launched the year 2000 as "the International Year for a Culture of Peace".[12]

In 1998 a meeting on "World Faiths and Development" was held at Lambeth Palace, London, jointly chaired by James D Wolfensohn, President of the World Bank, and by Dr George Carey, the Archbishop of Canterbury. From this emerged World Faiths Development Dialogue. This has brought together two actors on the development scene, the religious communities and the multilateral development agencies, which until now have gone their own way with considerable mutual suspicion. Now the hope is to connect those who possess expertise in technical issues and faith communities that stand closer than any others to the world's poorest people. Such a conscious step to forge an alliance should lead, in the words of Dr Carey and James D Wolfensohn, "to inspiration and learning among people from all sides and to ways of making some real changes in favor of those who most need them".[13]

In 2001, for the first time, The World Economic Forum - an independent foundation that engages business, political and other leaders of society seeking to improve the state of the world - invited religious leaders to share in their deliberations on globalization at Davos in Switzerland. It was recognized that "religious traditions have a unique contribution to offer ... particularly in emphasizing human values and the spiritual and moral dimension of economic and political life". [14]

The most striking example of the new seriousness with which

---

12 I am grateful to Dr Josef Boehle for permission to use this material from his as yet unpublished doctoral thesis for the University of Birmingham, "Inter-religious Co-operation in a Global Age", pp.63-91.
13 *World Faiths Development Dialogue, Exploring Dialogue,* A Report on Progress July 1998-December 2000, WFDD, 2001 p.3.
14 Press Release issued by the International Council of Christians and Jews, 31.1 2001.

international decision makers are taking the contribution of faith communities was the historic Millennium World Peace Summit of Religious and Spiritual Leaders, which met in UN General Assembly Hall in August 2000. This meeting, which issued a "Commitment to Global Peace", was of great symbolic significance, because previously, the United Nations had kept itself at some distance from faith communities because of the opposition of Communist countries - even though religious NGOs have, for many years, made a contribution at certain levels, in particular to specialist agencies.

The world needs a spiritual message

For some sixty years, as the existence of the UN testifies, the nations of the world have slowly recognized the limits of national sovereignty and the need for agreed international action on major issues of global concern. In the same way, although even more slowly, a "post-confessional and inter-religious world is coming into being. In other words, slowly and laboriously a multi-confessional ecumenical world society is coming into being".[15] But if religions are to have any real impact on shaping the future of this planet, they must come together far more quickly and effectively.

The new interest of many secular leaders in the moral dimension of life presents great opportunities for the world religions to share with a world in need, the spiritual riches of their traditions, and release the potential for peace that is at the heart of all great faiths. There are, however, dangers. One is that international bodies, instead of listening to the prophetic words of religious leaders, will try to give a cloak of respectability to their work by inviting a token presence of such leaders. Secondly, unless religious leaders recruit staff with the necessary expertise in relevant areas, they will have little to contribute. Leaders

---

15 Hans Küng, *Global Responsibility, In Search of an New World Ethic,* SCM Press 1991, p.49.

will also have to beware of attending so many international gatherings that they lose touch with local faith communities, so leaving the latter open to the influence of religious extremists. It is vital that, as international inter-religious co-operation increases, so local communities at the same time learn about other religions and meet members of them. Sometimes people complain that there are now too many interfaith groups. In fact there is more than enough work for all of them to do - locally, nationally and internationally - but that work needs to be better coordinated. The establishment of a network of International Interfaith Organizations, thanks to the efforts of the International Interfaith Centre at Oxford, is a welcome first step. Interfaith work requires more staff and far greater material resources. Just as the nations are reluctant to release finance for international activity so the religions prefer to spend money on themselves rather on co-operative ventures. But only together will the great faiths make available the spiritual resources that they have to offer for the healing of the world. Too easily, religion can be hi-jacked by those with a different agenda. Like human sexuality, the religious instinct can be the vehicle of great love and compassion or it can be perverted into cruel fanaticism.

The search for a new world order is essentially the search for a world society shaped by shared moral values. It is for the faiths to articulate more clearly and loudly the values that they share and to insist that they are relevant to political and economic life. Indeed unless international society is based on such values, the anarchy, terrorism and suffering in our contemporary world is bound to increase.

The role of religions during conflict

While faith communities can play an important role in reducing the likelihood of conflict, it is less obvious what they can do when conflict is actually raging. They can call for restraint, but President Bush and

Prime Minister Blair ignored such appeals by the Pope and other religious leaders prior to the Second Gulf War. Spiritual Leaders can urge people not to demonize the enemy. Sometimes people of faith can act as peace messengers or can be intermediaries in the preliminaries necessary to start formal peace talks. People of faith are also active in medical and relief work to help the victims of war. There is also a growing expertise in conflict resolution.

Even when ethnic and religious differences enflame hostilities, religious leaders, who have got to know each other, are increasingly speaking for reconciliation rather than championing the demands of their community.

The World Conference on *Religions for Peace* has been particularly active in South East Europe. Working with Muslim, Serbian Orthodox, Roman Catholic and Jewish leaders, it has facilitated the establishment of Inter-religious Councils in Bosnia-Herzegovina and Kosovo. It is hoped to launch such a council in Albania during 2005. The Inter-religious councils have helped to draft new laws on religious freedom, to educate the public through radio programs and have arranged inter-religious dialogues for reconciliation that include youth, women and religious leaders.

Kosovo, in mid-March 2004, saw its most serious outbreak of violence since the end of the 1999 conflict. The clashes started in the ethnically divided city of Kosovska Mitrovica, when a Serb man reported being shot at by a group of Albanians and ethnic Albanians blamed Serbs for the drowning of several Albanian children. Reports of the boys' deaths triggered a wave of rioting, looting and arson by ethnic Albanian mobs against the minority Serb population. Within 48 hours, 28 people were dead, 600 injured and 4,000 Serbs forced from their homes. Over 30 Orthodox churches and monasteries were destroyed. When a European Religions for Peace delegation visited Kosovo, they offered the Serbian Orthodox Bishop their condolences and, despite his grief and anger, Bishop Artemije reaffirmed his support for a multi-ethnic and multi-religious Kosovo. This, he said, required the right conditions for dialogue. The Catholic Bishop, Bishop Sopi, also condemned the violence and expressed his sorrow to the Serbian population.

In Belgrade, in reaction to the violence in Kosovo, a mob of nearly 2,000 people attacked a mosque and library, although Serbian and Jewish neighbors tried to dissuade them. The Serbian Orthodox Bishop also personally tried to stop the mob. Mufti Hamdija Jusufspahic thanked him for this, saying, "I don't know who caused the destruction, but I know who tried to help us". He also signed a burnt copy of the Qur'an and presented it to the Bishop.[16]

In Iraq, too, there are efforts to get the religious communities to work together. In July 2004, a representative group of Shi'a, Sunni and Christian leaders from Iraq met in Kyoto, Japan and agreed together to assist war-wounded Iraqi children – without regard for their religious, sectarian or ethnic identities. They also agreed to try to "overcome our injuries and sorrows, giving priority to the sufferings of the nation over our own".[17]

Despite all the news of conflict in Israel/Palestine, some interfaith meetings continue to take place regularly in Israel. There are also several Jewish groups, who campaign for justice for Palestinians. I vividly recall going to a Palestinian home that had twice been rebuilt by members of Rabbis for Human Rights, after it had twice been demolished by the military. Rabbis for Human Rights have planted many olive trees to replace those that have been cut down. They also try to ensure that Palestinians have legal help when they are in court.

The constructive efforts of those who work for peace in areas of conflict get little publicity and sometimes the violence of the conflict makes their work almost impossible. Even so, they sow the seeds of a more peaceful future.

---

16 World Conference of Religions for Peace, South East Europe Program Update, February 2005 and The Secretary General's Update, 15.5.04.
17 World Conference of Religions for Peace, The Secretary General's Update, August 2004.

Peace building after conflict

Practical help

When hostilities end, there is an enormous amount of work in continuing to care for those who have been injured or bereaved or rendered homeless by the conflict. Millions of people are refugees because of war. People of all faiths are actively involved in healing the wounds and heartache of the victims of violence and sowing the seeds of a better future. Abraham Garcia, the Mayan leader who himself suffered torture, has said, "there is no peace if there are people who walk barefoot, if there is no housing and no land".[18] Politicians insist that the "War Against Terror" must involve an active search for political, social and economic justice, but their actions seldom match their rhetoric.

Reconciliation and forgiveness

Practical help is vital, but equally important are efforts to help divided communities to free themselves from the bitterness of the past and to seek reconciliation. Without this, so-called peace agreements are superficial and short lived.

Archbishop Desmond Tutu has said, "there is no future without forgiveness". The truth of this was made clear to me when I visited Hiroshima. I was shown round by a Buddhist who as a child survived the terrible day on which the atomic bomb was dropped – a *hibakusha*. She told me honestly, but without bitterness, how her parents were killed and the pain and many operations she endured. When we came to the Peace Memorial we stood together in silent prayer. I was conscious of the terrible suffering caused by the dropping of the atomic bomb and she knew how much British prisoners had suffered at the hands of the Japanese. But in our shared penitence, we sensed a Divine peace, which overflows in compassion for all people.

---

18 Quoted in Marcus Braybrooke, 365 Meditations for a Peacefuk Heart and Perfect World, p. 296

Although it is right to seek justice for the victims of violence and oppression, there will be no lasting peace without mutual forgiveness. Mufti Camdzic, whose beautiful mosque in Banja Luka was destroyed during the ethnic cleansing of Bosnia has said "We can't forget; but we try to forgive and reconcile, to build again". [19]

I have no doubt about the importance of forgiveness, but I also hesitate to write about it as I have been spared the appalling suffering which has been inflicted on too many people. I have been to Auschwitz with a survivor; I have seen the terrible poverty of some people in India; and with members of the International Peace Council, I visited the remote village of Acteal in Mexico, where more than forty people were massacred just before Christmas 1997. Yet while I have tried to enter into the feelings of those who have endured great suffering, I am like a person sitting at the bedside of a loved one who is dying in pain. I can try to express my sympathy, I cannot know what she is feeling. Moreover none of us know what we would be able to forgive until we are put to the test.

Nonetheless, forgiveness and reconciliation are essential if there is to be a new future. The most striking recent example is in South Africa. Desmond Tutu, who chaired the Truth and Reconciliation Commission, has said, "We here in South Africa are a living example of how forgiveness may unite people".[20] The example was set by Nelson Mandela. When he was released after twenty-seven years in jail, he declared that his mission was to the victim and the victimizer. "Our miracle," Tutu continues, "almost certainly would not have happened without the willingness of people to forgive, exemplified spectacularly in the magnanimity of Nelson Mandela".[21] Despite this, it was recognized that the evils of the apartheid era had to be faced, before reconciliation was possible.

---

19 *Ibid,* p.316
20 Desmond Tutu in *Exploring Forgiveness,* Eds. Robert D. Enright and Joanna North, University of Wisconsin Press, 1998, p.xiii.
21 *Ibid.*

The poet Edwin Muir wrote that if we fail to face the evils of the past, "long since rusted knives" stab us from behind and "revengeful dust rises up to haunt us".[22] A general amnesty, which would have amounted to amnesia, was rejected, but also the Nuremberg option of the victors putting the vanquished on trial. The participation of white South Africans in the new nation was essential to its economic development. A third option - a Truth and Reconciliation Commission - was agreed. This was not like the one in Chile that was behind closed doors and on condition that General Pinochet and other members of the military junta were given amnesty. South Africa's third way was "the granting of amnesty to individuals in exchange for a full disclosure relating to the crime for which amnesty was being sought".[23]

There are many dimensions to forgiveness and these are increasingly being studied.[24] Forgiveness is essentially a religious concept, although there are important differences of emphasis between religions. Forgiveness may have been possible in part in South Africa because of the strength of the Christian church in that country. When I was in South Africa in 1999, I met with some people who had been dispossessed when District Six, a vibrant multi-racial community in the heart of Cape Town, was bulldozed under the apartheid regime. I asked two of the colored women what they felt about their oppressors. "We must forgive them" they said, "because Jesus forgives".

The new relationship of Jews and Christians, as already mentioned, is another example of the power of forgiveness. This would not have been possible without the willingness of Christians to acknowledge past anti-Jewish teaching, prejudice and persecution and ask forgiveness. This dimension seems to have been in short supply in the peace process in Israel/Palestine and in Northern Ireland. The

---

22 From Edwin Muir's poem "The Wheel", quoted by Donald W Shriver in *Exploring Forgiveness*, p.131
23 Desmond Tutu *No Future Without Forgiveness*, Rider 1999, p.34
24 For example by the International Forgiveness Institute, PO Box 6153, at Madison, WI 53716-0153, or the Forgiveness Project in London, www.theforgivenessproject.com

release of convicted prisoners in Northern Ireland was extremely painful
to the relatives of their victims. Some accepted it was a necessary price
for peace, but it might have been more acceptable if there had been
some expression of regret for the past. When I asked some released
prisoners in Northern Ireland how they now saw the past, their answer
was that bad things happen in war. A remarkable exception to this has
been the effort of Jo Berry, whose father, Sir Anthony Berry, a Member
of Parliament, was killed in the IRA Brighton bombing. She made
contact with the man responsible, Patrick Magee, to try to understand
what led him to such violence. "It's about shared responsibility in terms
of politics and history," she said. She recognized that until both the
victim and the perpetrator acknowledge the evil that has been done,
both remain prisoners of a cruel past. "Meeting him has helped me to
heal," she says. "I experience empathy and in that moment there is no
judgment".[25]

Forgiveness, which is emphasized in many religious traditions,
may be the only way to help people break free of past hatred. In the final
chapter of his book *No Future Without Forgivenes,* Desmond Tutu
describes a visit to Rwanda a year after the massacre of at least half a
million people. He argued that revenge only sowed the seeds of
reciprocal revenge in the future. The President of Rwanda said the
people were willing to forgive, but even Jesus had declared that the devil
could not be forgiven.[26] Tutu, however, held that no atrocity was beyond
the possibility of God's pardon. Many Jews, with the memory of the
Holocaust, and some Christians would not agree with Tutu. He
recognizes that a papering over the cracks is a cheap peace that is no
peace. "True reconciliation exposes the awfulness, the abuse, the pain,
the degradation, the truth ... People are not being asked to forget ...
Forgiveness means abandoning your right to pay back the perpetrator in
his own coin, but it is a loss which liberates the victim".[27] He ends the

---

25 "Don't Forget to Forgive", *The Times*, (Body and Soul) 5.2.05, pp.16-17.
26 The basis for the President's assertion is not clear.
27 *No Future Without Forgiveness*, pp.218-9.

book by saying, "God wants to show that there is life after conflict and repression - that because of forgiveness, there is a future".[28]

It is not easy to help those who have been deeply hurt to let go the injury. It will require great courage for religious leaders to call for reconciliation instead of revenge, and to affirm the common humanity of oppressed and oppressors.

Our shared humanity

Forgiveness is vital, but a sense of our shared humanity is also essential.

A particularly moving happening is described by Yevtushenko in his biography. His mother took him back to Moscow in 1941, where he saw German war prisoners being marched through the streets. "There I saw our enemies for the first time", he wrote. "If my memory is right, nearly 20,000". The watching crowd were mostly women. "Every one of them must have had a father or a husband, a brother or a son killed by the Germans". They were gazing with hatred as the column of prisoners approached. "They saw the German soldiers, thin, unshaven, wearing dirty blood stained bandages, hobbling on crutches or leaning on the shoulders of their comrades; the soldiers walked with their heads down". There was silence in the street, the sound only of shuffling boots and crutches hitting the ground. Then, wrote Yevtushenko, "I saw an elderly woman in broken-down boots push herself forward and touch a policeman's shoulder, saying, 'Let me through ...' She went up to the column, took from inside her coat something wrapped in a colored handkerchief and unfolded it. It was a crust of black bread. She pushed it awkwardly into the pocket of a soldier, so exhausted that he was tottering on his feet. And now suddenly from every side women were running towards the soldiers pushing into their hands bread, cigarettes, whatever they had ... The soldiers were no longer enemies. They were people".[29]

---

28 *No Future Without Forgiveness*, p.230.
29 Yevgeny Yevtushenko, *A Precocious Autobiography*, Collins 1963, pp. 24-5, quoted by Brian Frost in *The Politics of Peace*, Darton, Longman and Todd 1991, pp. 15-16.

This sense of our shared humanity is vividly expressed by Thich Nhat Hahn, a Vietnamese Buddhist peace worker, in a poem entitled, "Please call Me by My True Names":

> *I am the child in Uganda, all skin and bones,*
> *my legs as thin as bamboo sticks,*
> *and I am the arms merchant, selling deadly*
> *weapons to Uganda.*
>
> *I am the 12-year-old girl, refugee*
> *on a small boat,*
> *who throws herself into the ocean after*
> *being raped by a sea pirate,*
> *and I am the pirate, my heart not yet capable*
> *of seeing and loving.*
>
> *I am a member of the politburo, with*
> *plenty of power in my hands,*
> *and I am the man who has to pay his*
> *"debt of blood" to my people,*
> *dying slowly in a forced labour camp....*
>
> *Please call me by my true names,*
> *so I can wake up,*
> *and so the door of my heart can be left open,*
> *the door of compassion.*[30]

Conclusion

Edwin Muir, whose poem "The Wheel" I have already quoted, says in it that history plagues us like a relentless wheel. Who, he asks, can "set

---

30 Thich Nhat Hahn, *Being Peace*, Parallax Press Berkeley 1987, pp.63-64.

a new mark" or "circumvent history?"[30] I believe it is possible, I believe that the religions of the world have begun to overcome past misunderstanding, bitterness and hostility, to build a new relationship, based on reconciliation and co-operation. This can be a sign of hope to the nations and to divided and warring communities, but only if like Joseph and his brothers, we weep on each others' shoulders,[31] admit the pain that we have consciously or unconsciously caused to each other, and with God's grace start afresh.

In 1983, as I have said, I attended the Vancouver Assembly of the World Council of Churches. The British had just been at war with the Argentineans over the Falklands. I found that at the opening ceremony I was sitting quite near some Christians from Argentina. I knew that I could not in good conscience take part in the Assembly until I had made my peace with those who were there from Argentina. We wept and prayed together for those who had been injured and bereaved in that war. If people of faith can learn to say sorry, they may help nations, which have been torn apart by violence, to do the same. But to do that, they need to draw on the inner resources of their faith. It is as we become people of peace that we help to create the culture of peace. The Japanese scientist, poet and mystic, Dr Takashi Nagai, who grew up in Nagasaki, through his own suffering and meditation recognized that "loving our neighbors as we love ourselves" is the only way to peace. Non-violence has to start in the heart, because that's where killing starts. "Go to the mountains and meditate", Dr Nagai told enquirers. "In the hurly-burly of the city, you rush around in circles. But the Blue Mountains are immovable".[32]

---

30 From Edwin Muir's poem "The Wheel".
31 Genesis, 45:15.
32 Marcus Braybrooke, *365 Meditations for a Peaceful Heart and a Peaceful World,* p.315.

GLOBALIZATION: CURSE OR CURE?

GLOBALIZATION: CURSE OR CURE?

"The hand withheld"

Vegetarian meals at Madras Christian College, where I was a student forty years ago, were served on plantain (banana) leaves. When we had finished eating, the leaves were collected and thrown onto the rubbish heap. Birds gathered, as I expected, to pick over the leaves, but I was shocked the first time I saw young boys turning over the remains, hoping to find a few grains of rice.

That scene, which haunts my memory, is also a symbol of the gross inequalities in our world. Those of us who have enough to eat so easily forget the millions of people condemned to a life of hunger and degradation. This Litany from Calcutta expresses something of what they have to put up with:

> *Lord teach us to hate our poverty of spirit.*
> *Poverty is*
> *a knee-level view from your bit of pavement;*
> *a battered, upturned cooking pot and countable ribs,*
> *coughing from your steel-banded lungs, alone,*
> *with your face to the wall;*
> *shrunken breast and a three year old who cannot stand;*
> *the ringed fingers, the eyes averted and a five-paise piece*
> *in your palm;*
> *smoking the* babus' *cigarette butts to quieten the fiend*
> *in your belly;*

a husband without a job, without a square meal a day,
without energy, without hope;
being at the mercy of everyone further up the ladder
because you are a threat to their self-respect;
- a hut of tins and rags and plastic bags,
in a warren of huts you cannot stand up in,
where your neighbors live at one arm's length across the lane;
- a man who cries out in silence;
nobody listening, for everyone's talking;
- the prayer withheld
the hand withheld; yours and mine.[1]

It is important not to forget the misery of the individual (so often a woman or a child) condemned to hunger and malnutrition. When we think about global statistics we need to be aware of the size of the problem. Here are some shocking statistics: "Half the people on earth live on less than two dollars a day, a billion people on less than a dollar a day. A billion people go to bed hungry every night – and a billion and a half – one quarter of the people on earth never get a clean glass of water. One woman dies every minute in childbirth".[2] In twenty-three countries, half or more of the adult population is illiterate.[3] The situation is aggravated by the spread of HIV/AIDS. Two and a half million people were expected to die of AIDS in the year 2004.[4] The gap is getting worse and there is real concern that the Millennium Development Goals, which are printed as an Appendix, will not be achieved.

---

1 Quoted in *1,000 World Prayers*, ed. Marcus Braybrooke, John Hunt Publishing, 2003, p. 311.
2 From President Clinton's 2002 Richard Dimbleby Lecture Quoted in John Dunning, *Making Globalization Good*, Oxford University Press 2003, p.171.
3 Quoted in John Dunning, *Making Globalization Good*, p.219.
4 Figures quoted by Bono in *Millennium Challenges for Development and Faith Institutions*, ed. Katherine Marshall and Richard Marsh, The World Bank, 2003, p.13.

The size of the problem is staggering: but even so it is a matter of priorities and the choices we and others make. During the Vietnam War it cost the USA about £130,000 for each Vietnamese person who was killed. To keep a Vietnamese child alive and to educate him or her would have cost less than £75 a year.[5]

Find God in the poor

The Buddha said, 'May my heart lend its ear to every cry of pain.'[6]

Teachers of many faiths insist that the cry of the poor is the voice of God. There are many stories of God taking the disguise of a beggar. The Hindu poet Tulsidas wrote:

> *Treat all people well.*
> *Perhaps to your surprise,*
> *The one whom you are meeting*
> *Is God in some disguise.*[7]

Jesus, who in the nineteen sixties was often called "the man for others", identified himself with the poor. In his parable of the sheep and the goats, Jesus told of a king, who divided the good people from the bad, in the same way that a shepherd divides his sheep from his goats. To the good people on his right, the king said:

> "You have my Father's blessing; come, enter and
> possess the kingdom that has been made ready
> for you since the world was made. For when I
> was hungry, you gave me food; when thirsty, you
> gave me drink, when I was a stranger you took
> me into your home, when naked you clothed me;
> when I was ill you came to my help, when in

---

5 *Go, Know and Live,* ed Anders Akerlund and Michael Proctor, SCM Press, 1970, p.49.
6 *1,000 World Prayers,* p.311.
7 *1,000 World Prayers,* p.313.

prison you visited me". When the righteous
questioned this, the king replied, "Anything you
did for my brothers here, however humble, you
did for me".[8]

Similarly, the Sufi Jalal Al-Din Rumi has God say, "Yea, a favorite and chosen slave of mine fell sick. I am he. Consider well: his infirmity is my infirmity, his sickness is my sickness".[9]

Many recent spiritual teachers have also stressed that the true service of God is not in a place of worship but in caring for those in need. Gandhi espoused the cause of the poor and outcastes, whom he called *harijans* or "children of God". Likewise, the Indian poet Rabindranath Tagore wrote:

> *Leave this chanting and singing and telling of beads!*
> *Whom dost thou worship in this lonely dark corner of a*
> *temple*
> *With doors all shut?*
> *Open thine eyes and see thy God is not before thee!*
> *He is where the tiller is tilling the hard ground*
> *and where the path maker is breaking stones...*
> *Put off thy holy mantle and even like him*
> *Come down on the dusty soil!...*
> *Meet him and stand by him in toil and in sweat of thy*
> *brow*[10].

Part of the response to the terrible poverty in which so many people live is how we ourselves live and how much we give to charity. That is a matter for the conscience of each one of us. The bigger and

---

8 Matthew 25, 33-40.
9 *1,000 World Prayers*, p.312.
10 *1,000 World Prayers*, p.310-311.

more difficult task is to challenge the forces of globalization and to try to control them and use them for good.

This should be a priority for members of all religions.[11] Sadly, that is not the case. A recent poll of Evangelical church members in the USA showed that only six per cent thought they should be doing more about the AIDS emergency.[12] "I might even say," wrote Bono, who is lead singer and lyricist for the well known band U, "that God is on his knees, begging us to act, to get up off our behinds – and I include myself in this – and take the fight against world poverty to a new level".[13]

But can religions speak on this vital issue with a united voice? Despite the passages quoted above that God is to be met in the service of the poor, there are significant differences within and between religions in their attitudes to material possessions and therefore to wealth creation, economic growth and Globalization.

What do we mean by globalization?

Globalization is a word with many meanings. It "has been used to describe the way the rationalist philosophy and way of life, which developed in Western Europe, has been spreading all around the world. It could equally well be described as the modernization or Westernization (some call it the Americanization) of the world".[14] It is understandable that some people in Africa and Asia see this as a threat to their traditional culture and religion. Few people would want globalization if it means a monochrome culture – and of course satellite

---

11 Paul Knitter has argued this forcefully in *One Earth, Many Religions*, Orbis 1995, see especially pp.56ff.

12 Bono refers to this in *Millennium Challenges for Development and Faith Institutions*, p.13.

13 Bono in *Millennium Challenges for Development and Faith Institutions*, p.13.

14 Claire Disbrey, *Listening to People of Other Faiths*, Bible Reading Fellowship, 2004, p.20.

television and the spread of Coca Cola and McDonalds make this a real danger. But globalization is more than Westernization, it also implies the spread of capitalism worldwide, which critics say is to the benefit of the rich nations at the expense of the poorer countries and of the environment. This is why globalization often gets a bad press. "A ragbag alliance of protectionists, trade unions, anarchists, leftists, environmentalists, animal rights protesters and concerned citizens has authored one of the grand narratives of our time: globalization is bad".[15] But such a condemnation is too sweeping.

It is helpful to distinguish "globalization" from "the global market place" and "global capitalism", although these three entities are often misleadingly treated as if they were one and the same. Globalization is "connectivity of individuals and institutions across the globe". The global market place refers to the flow of goods, services and assets across national boundaries. The concept of global capitalism points to the network of cross-border relationships that link a large number of distinctive national or regional capitalist economies.[16] It is potentially a world economic system. It is primarily global capitalism that will be discussed here.

Global capitalism is based on the liberal economic belief that the market is autonomous. The market is thought to comprise rational, maximizing individuals, who as buyers or sellers are free to choose. The greater the freedom, the more competition there will be and the more efficient the market will become. This economic view is in contrast to the protectionism and trade barriers that aggravated the Great Depression of early twentieth century and also in contrast to the centralized state-managed economies of Communist countries. With the fall of the Berlin wall and the collapse of Communism, capitalism

---

15 Charles Leadbeater, extract from his book *Up the Down Escalator: Why Global Pessimists Are Wrong* , Viking/Peguin, 2002, in *The Times*, 26.6.02.
16 John Dunning, *Making Globalisation Good*, pp. 12-13.

has now become the dominant economic system in most parts of the world. Multi-national companies operate across national boundaries, thereby eroding the nation state. The amazing growth of the internet and e-commerce has revolutionized communications. Yet, although the spread of capitalism has increased the wealth of many nations, the very poor have been excluded from this and are often worse off, traditional cultures are threatened and the environment is in danger. Jonathan Sacks, the British Chief Rabbi highlights the promise and threat of globalization when he says, "Global capitalism heralds the prospect of vast amelioration of the human condition. Equally it threatens inequalities that will eventually become unsustainable and cultural vandalism that will become unbearable".[17]

Rather than rejecting globalization *per se*, we should strive to ensure that all people enjoy its benefits, while we seek to minimize its harmful effects. I agree with those whose aim is responsible global capitalism or globalization for the common good. I do not myself see globalization as necessarily an evil. I doubt also whether the technological developments that have made it possible to cross the world in twenty-four hours and to communicate instantly to other continents can be reversed, even if we were to wish that this were possible. It has advantages and disadvantages. I largely agree with Hans Küng that globalization is unavoidable, ambivalent, unpredictable, and, I hope, controllable. Globalization, as Hans Küng says, is "not a conspiracy of the Americans, the Japanese or some dark powers, but a result of the technological and economic development of modern Europe".[18] Economic and technological unification can add to the richness of our life. Think of the variety of fruits and vegetables, flown in from around the world, to be found in most supermarkets, although

---

17 Jonathan Sacks, *The Dignity of Difference*, Continuum, 2002, p.97.
18 Hans Küng, *A Global Ethic for Global Politics and Economics*, SCM Press 1997, p.160.

their production may distort the local economy and be environmentally damaging. The telephone, let alone e-mail, has transformed communications, but this again emphasizes the divisions in our world. Fifty per cent of the people in the world have never made a telephone call in their life. I rejoice at the possibilities of travel that I never dreamed of as a child, but what is the environmental damage of jet travel and exotic holidays?

My own hope is that as people of the world are brought together technologically and economically, so they will come together spiritually and this has been one of my motivations for interfaith work. More than three thousand years ago,[19] the ancient Iranian prophet Zoroaster voiced the ideal of a single human family and this vision has been expressed by seers and prophets of many religions in every century. The growth of a world community is part of the dynamic of history, which at an earlier stage led to the creation of nation states and perhaps is part of the purpose of God to create a new humanity.

The development of a world community is indeed essential if globalization is to be controlled and to be for the good of humanity as a whole. Kofi Anan, Secretary General of the UN, insists that the challenges that face humankind transcend national boundaries. "Issues such as environment, crime, terrorism, and corruption carry no passports".[20] These issues also transcend religious frontiers. If we are to tackle the great problems facing human kind, which are essentially moral and spiritual problems, we need to draw on the wisdom of **all** the great religions. As the philosopher and sometime President of India Dr Sarvepalli Radhakrishnan said some years ago, "We need a spiritual faith which may serve as a basis for the new world order".[21] I do not see the interfaith movement as an attempt to impose a Western morality or

---

19 Zoroaster is traditionally dated to about 6,000 BCE by Zoroastrians. Many Western scholars used to date him to about 600 BCE, but more recent scholars such as M. Boyce and G. Gnoli suggest he lived about 1200 BCE.
20 Message of Kofi Anan to the 9th International Anti-Corruption Conference in Durban in 1999, quoted in the Newsletter of the 10th International Anti-Corruption Conference, Prague, 8.10.01, p.3.
21 S. Radhakrishnan, *Religion in a Changing World*, George, Allen and Unwin, 1967, p.11.

ideology on the rest of the world or a human effort to create a One World Religion or religious Esperanto, but as a sharing of the spiritual riches of the great communities of faith. It is a spiritual counterpart of the technological and scientific coming together of humanity and essential to ensure that the possibilities of scientific advance are a blessing and not a curse.[22]

I shall return to the question of how we can ensure that globalization is for the benefit of all people and also to the contribution of people of faith to making this happen, but because religions are ambivalent in their attitudes to wealth, we have first to ask whether wealth itself is a blessing or a snare?

Is economic growth desirable?

Global capitalism assumes a certain pattern of economic activity that fosters human enterprise but at the same time encourages competition and greed. Within and between religions there are different responses to the dangers of globalization. The issue is whether the key problem of globalization is the way in which economic growth is created and distributed or whether the promotion of economic growth is itself open to question. If economic growth is a legitimate human goal, the question becomes how do we stop it becoming a tyrant or an all-devouring monster? If economic growth itself is the problem, how do we root out the greed that fuels the rampant contemporary economic activity?

The Hindu reformer Swami Agnivesh puts the dilemma very clearly:

---

22 John B Chethimattam has said that 'the very label of a Global Ethic smacks of an imperialist plot to continue imperialism's dominance on the majority of humanity through specious moral preaching', in *Visions of an Interfaith Future*, ed David and Celia Storey, International Interfaith Centre, Oxford, 1994, pp.115-6.

> There are two radically different approaches
> to dealing with the issue of human greed.
> The first is to put in place checks and
> balances so that the predatory and
> exploitative instincts in human nature do
> not become socially subversive. This
> approach is centered in law ...
>
> The second approach, however, rejects this
> assumption and assumes that the persistence
> of greed and its power over individuals and
> societies stems from a materialistic
> worldview. If lust for material acquisition
> can be tempered with love for one's fellow
> human beings and accountability to God, it
> becomes possible to deal with the problem
> of greed effectively.[23]

The second approach, as Swami Agnivesh makes clear, requires a radical change of view so that instead of competition we "promote a spirit of caring and sharing. It is fostering a culture of universal responsibility, responsible stewardship of Earth's resources and a sense of global kinship that discourages thriving at the expense of one's fellow beings as an ugly and undesirable agenda".[24]

This, however, means challenging the materialistic assumptions of a secular society and the competitiveness that is inherent in capitalism. It demands "an alternate set of perspectives and goals".[25] In one sense, this approach rejects the present consensus just as much as does the fundamentalist protest, but it offers a radically different answer based on a unitive spirituality.

---

23 Swami Agnivesh in *Subverting Greed*, eds. Paul Knitter and Chandra Muzaffar, Orbis 2002, pp.50-51.
24 Swami Agnivesh in *Subverting Greed*, p.50.
25 Swami Agnivesh in *Subverting Greed*, p.51.

"Do religions offer such an alternative to the present global economy?" Much traditional teaching about money deals with individual rather than corporate behavior. Religions, do not, therefore, have ready made answers to the challenges of global capitalism. Dr Chandra Muzaffar, who is President of the Malaysian-based International Movement for a Just World answers his own question like this. "If by an alternative one means a complete economic system with a guiding philosophy, structures, modalities, and goals, no scripture has the answer".[26] David Loy of Bunkyo University in Japan also says that none of the various religions of Asia "has anything to say about the challenge of capitalism, global or otherwise".[27]

The attitudes of religions to wealth creation

There are differences of emphasis within and between religions, as Swami Agnivesh suggests. Jews, Muslims, Sikhs and some Christians, as we shall see, usually consider wealth, honestly earned and fairly distributed, as a blessing of God to be enjoyed as such. Most Hindus and Buddhists and some Christians, on the other hand, are more hesitant and warn that money may distract the soul from salvation.

In comparing the attitudes of religions to wealth creation, I shall highlight the differences by giving special attention to two books: *Dignity of Difference* by the Chief Rabbi, Dr Jonathan Sacks, and *Enough is Enough* by Dr John Taylor, a former Anglican bishop of Winchester, who had previously worked in Africa. The difference between them reflects the difference that the Catholic writer Michael Novak identifies between the Jewish and Christian approaches to this subject:

---

26 Chandra Muzaffar, *Subverting Greed*, p.159.
27 David R Loy, *Making Globalization Good*, p.232.

In both its prophetic and rabbinic traditions Jewish thought has always felt comfortable with a certain well ordered worldliness. Jewish thought has had a candid orientation toward private property, commercial activity, markets, and profits, whereas Catholic thought – articulated from an early period chiefly among priests and monks – has persistently tried to direct the attention of its adherents beyond the activities and interest of this world to the next.[28]

Judaism

The Dignity of Difference

Jonathan Sacks' *Dignity of Difference* is a good example of Jewish thought. He makes clear that in Judaism prosperity is a sign of God's blessing and that asceticism and self-denial have little place in Jewish spirituality. The third-century sage, Rav said, "In the world to come we will face judgment for every legitimate pleasure we denied ourselves in this life".[29] Sacks also points out that a recurring theme in the book of Deuteronomy is "You shall rejoice in all the good things the Lord your God has given to you and your household".[30]

Sacks' approach to what he calls the market economy is, therefore, essentially positive. He argues that the reason why Europe's economic development leapt ahead in the nineteenth century was because of the Judeo-Christian ethic.[31] This ethic includes, first, respect

---

28 M. Novak, *The Hemisphere of Liberty*, American Enterprise Institute, Washington DC, 1992, p.64.
29 Jerusalem Talmud, *Kiddushin*, 4.12.
30 Deuteronomy 26:11.
31 Sacks bases his argument on David Landes' book, *The Wealth and Poverty of Nations*, Little, Brown and Co, 1998.

for property rights, whereas in many ancient cultures all property belonged to the ruler. Secondly, the Bible also insisted that every individual is valuable in his or her own right, because made in the image of God. In many ancient cultures, on the other hand, it was the king who was regarded as divine and as the representative or embodiment of the gods. Thirdly, as Psalm 128 says, "When you eat the fruit of your own labor, you shall be happy and it will be good for you". Work allows a person to share in the creativity of God. The thirteenth-century commentator Rabbenu Bachya said, "The active participation of man in the creation of his own wealth is a sign of his spiritual greatness".[32] Moses Maimonides also insisted that rabbinic scholars should earn their own living.[33] Indeed Rav had already said, "Flay carcasses in the marketplace and do not say; 'I am a priest and a great man and it is beneath my dignity'."[34] This contrasts with the classical view that manual labor was below the dignity of the scholar. In the Greek myths, the gods did not work and Aristotle called the life of commerce "ignoble and inimical to excellence".[35] A similar disparaging view of manual work is reflected in the traditional Indian caste system.

Judaism sees wealth as a blessing. Therefore, "the economic growth produced by globalization and information technology has *religious* significance," says Sacks, "first and foremost because of the degree to which, more than any previous order, it allows us to alleviate poverty. Throughout its history, Judaism resisted any attempt to romanticize, rationalize or anaesthetize the pain of hunger, starvation or need".[36] Judaism, Sacks adds, has recognized that the motivation for economic endeavor may be selfish – prompted by "the evil inclination" – but that its outcome is beneficial. The Book of Ecclesiastes says, "I saw that all labor and all achievement spring from man's envy of his

---

32 Rabbenu Bachya, *Kad hakemac,* quoted in Meir Tamari, *With All Your Possessions: Jewish Ethics and Economic Life,* Free Press, New York, 1987, p.31.
33 Moses Maimonides, *Mishnah Torah,* Laws of Theft, 6:8-11.
34 Jerusalem Talmud, *Berakhot,* 9.2.
35 Aristotle, *The Politics,* para. 1328 b 41, 1988, p.168.
36 Jonathan Sacks, *The Dignity of Difference,* Continuum, 2002, p.97.

neighbor".[37] Dr Sacks[38] is well aware that wealth today is unfairly distributed and that this undermines social solidarity. Sacks summarizes the appalling inequalities in our world society and within developed societies. We are sadly familiar with these injustices, so I need not repeat them here. Sacks seeks an answer to these injustices in the Jewish concept of *Tzedakah*, which combines charity and justice or what he calls "redistributive justice". Judaism, Sacks suggests, "represents a highly distinctive approach to the idea of equality, namely that it is best served not by equality of income or wealth, nor even of opportunity ... (but) by ensuring equal dignity or 'human honor', *kavod habriyot*, to each of its members".[39]

Islam

Islam's approach to wealth is similar to that of Judaism. I.R.Al-Faruqi wrote, "Every Muslim desires and plans to become a 'millionaire' if he or she takes Islam seriously".[40] He insists that money should be fairly

---

37 Ecclesiastes 4:4.

38 Rabbi Dr Norman Solomon takes a similarly positive, if more nuanced view, towards wealth creation. He writes:

Religious people do not identify progress with increased provision of material goods and services. Nevertheless, most religions teach us to look after the poor, to heal the sick, to provide food and shelter for those in need, and to pursue justice. All of these counsels demand material and personal resources. Even from a religious point of view, therefore, we are justified in regarding the growth of wealth and material resources as a major element in human progress toward the kind of world we believe God wants us to strive for.

Based on this idea that material wealth serves God, the creation of wealth becomes not only acceptable but desirable. However, the desirability of the creation of wealth raises two major issues for religious people. At the individual, personal level is it possible to engage in the pursuit of wealth without succumbing to greed and selfishness? Second, at all levels of society, right up to the global level, there is the vexing problem of distribution: can wealth be distributed equitably?

Solomon points out that although the rabbis saw real poverty as an affliction, "The rabbis condemned the pursuit of wealth for its own sake as a major evil, responsible through envy and greed for human conflict and for turning people away from God. Jewish moralistic literature discourages individuals from engaging more than absolutely necessary in commerce; one should seek one's basic needs, that is all".

39 J. Sacks, *The Dignity of Difference*, p. 120 See also *Making Globalisation Good*, p.222.

40 I R Al-Faruqi, *Islam*, Argus Communications 1979, p.57.

earned and not accumulated by cheating and exploitation of natural resources. Further Muslims should provide for the poor both by paying *Zakat,* which prescribes that two and one-half per cent of a person's total wealth is distributed to the needy, and by other charitable giving or *sadaqah.* Muslims, Al-Faruqi says, "believe that God commands them to produce wealth so that all may live and prosper. They thank God if their efforts succeed, and they bear it patiently if they fail".[41] The Qur'an provides an explicit incentive for economic enterprise when it says, "When the call to prayer is proclaimed on Friday, hasten earnestly to the remembrance of God and leave off business ... and when the prayer is finished then may you disperse through the land, and seek the bounty of God".[42] Professor Khurshid Ahmed of the Islamic Foundation at Markfield, near Leicester, says the same, "Wealth is not a dirty word; in fact wealth creation is a desirable goal, subject only to moral values and imperatives".[43]

All wealth and possessions are a gift and a trust from God, not by right or simply due to one's own efforts, but from God's beneficence. There is no ascetic tradition of monks and nuns in Islam, but the Qur'an warns that the greed which leads to unlimited accumulation of possessions erodes a person's religious belief and leads him astray. "Woe to (him) who pileth wealth and layeth it by, thinking that his wealth would make him last".[44] Islam, says Dr Ameer Ali of the University of Western Australia, "is not against the profit motive, the cardinal principle of free-market ideology; but it is not willing to allow the profit motive to determine human progress".[45]

Islam deplores the economic injustice in the world. It opposes any exploitation of an individual or a group by others and insists that every person is entitled to the fruits of his or her labor. "To every person

---

41 *Ibid.*
42 Qur'an 62, 9-10.
43 Khurshid Ahmed in *Making Globalization Good,* p.192.
44 Qur'an, 104, 1-3.
45 Ameer Ali in *Subverting Greed,* p.147.

whatever gain he/she has earned; against every person whatever loss he/she has earned".[46] Islam sees economic growth and material advancement as only a means to an end and not an end in itself. As a result, on several grounds, Islam from its economic perspective, is critical of globalization. Dr Ameer Ali summarizes these concerns as follows:

> An increasing concentration of wealth in the hands of the few and the yawning gap between the rich and the poor.
>
> The short-termism and speculation that dominate modern financial markets.
>
> The reckless destruction to the environment caused by modern techniques of production.
>
> The rising trend of consumerism.
>
> The passionate obsession with economic growth.[47]

For Judaism and Islam then, to put it briefly, there is no problem with honest wealth creation. The question is how that wealth is used.

Like Judaism and Islam, Sikhism also has no place for asceticism and was also critical of the Hindu caste system. Guru Nanak lived as a householder and rejected the Hindu *sannyasi's* way of renunciation and austerity. "He alone has found the right way, who eats what he earns through toil and shares his earnings with the needy", says the Adi Granth.[48] The scriptures recognize that both wealth and poverty can cause anxiety. "Those who have money have the anxiety of greed: those without money have the anxiety of poverty".[49] Riches, the scriptures say, should be honestly earned and not result from exploitation of the poor.

---

46 Qur'an 2, 286.
47 Ameer Ali in *Subverting Greed,* p.148.
48 Adi Granth, 1245.
49 Adi Granth, 1019.

Further, wealth should not distract its owners from life's spiritual purpose. In comparison with *Nam* (God's name), wealth is nothing. Sikhism's stress on the equality of all people, demonstrated by the *langar* or free kitchen which is open to all people, means that relief of poverty is regarded as a duty.

Christianity

Some Christians take a similar view. A new report for the British churches concludes that "under the right conditions, economic growth can serve God's purposes".[50] The Christian economist Brian Griffiths of Goldman Sachs International takes a similar view and is positive about globalization, although he is well aware of its shortcomings. He recognizes the contradictions that exist at a theological level between different Christian approaches. "These range from creation ethics, which grounds an ethical response in the nature of the created world and the moral principles contained in the Decalogue; to the ethics of the kingdom, which focuses on radical change brought about by the life and teaching of Jesus; and to situation ethics, which rejects any attempt to apply universally valid and prescriptive rules, and emphasizes in their place the uniqueness of each situation and the need for a response based on love and not rules".[51] Griffiths continues: "The confirmation by Jesus of the moral law of the Old Testament is, in terms of economic life, an endorsement of its teaching regarding wealth creation, the freedom of exchange, the ownership of private property, the obligations which ownership brings, and the importance of economic justice".[52] Jesus, he adds, "never questioned that the material world was anything other than

---

50 *Prosperity With a Purpose – Christians and the Ethics of Affluence*, Churches Together in Britain and Ireland, 2005, quoted in *The Sunday Times*, 6.2.05, p.2.
51 Brian Griffiths in *Making Globalization Good*, p.161.
52 Brian Griffiths in *Making Globalization Good*, p.164.

the blessing of God, but stressed that our material life needed to be set in the context of the spiritual life, and touched lightly. His mission was to preach the good news to the poor, the hungry, the excluded, something the rich would find difficult to comprehend, because of their self-assurance and self-satisfaction". [53]

From a Christian standpoint, Griffiths rejects the arguments of F A Hayek that the market is autonomous. He insists that "if global capitalism were allowed to develop within a free market Hayekian framework it would suffer from three weaknesses: there would be no external standards of what was right and wrong, just and unjust, moral and immoral, by which its results could be judged; there would be no guarantee that even in the absence of outside intervention, globalization would be a benign process; and there would be no assurance that in a free society left to itself, we could count on an evolution of moral beliefs to generate values which would continue to underpin the market order".[54]

Griffiths also rejects the views of those Christians who condemn capitalism *per se* such as Bishop Newbigin who wrote, '"The capitalist system is powered by the unremitting stimulation of covetousness". [55]

Griffiths claims that research shows clearly that economic growth benefits the poor, that more rapid growth in developing countries is associated with trade liberalization and increased foreign investment, and that globalization has not, on average, resulted in greater inequality in the distribution of income in developing countries. On average, the incomes of the poorest twenty per cent of the population have grown at the same rate as the GDP. He makes clear, however, that globalization has done nothing to help the *really* poor that live in countries which are marginal to the world economy.[56] Griffiths

---

53 Brian Griffiths *in Making Globalization Good, p.164*.
54 Brian Griffiths *in Making Globalization Good p.168*.
55 Brian Griffiths *in Making Globalization Good, p.168*, quoting Leslie Newbigin, *Foolishness to the Greeks, SPCK, 1986, p.113*.
56 Brian Griffiths in *Making Globalization Good*, p.171.

makes specific suggestions about how global capitalism needs to be reformed. Even so, his main conclusions are that global capitalism has moral legitimacy.[57]

Other Christians are very critical of those Christians, particularly middle-class North Americans, who buy into capitalism. They are, according to Sallie McFague of the Vancouver School of Theology, captives of the neo-classical market model, with its ideology of greed.[58] By contrast, the critics of globalization, like St Francis, believe that the only way to care for the poor is to identify with them. "The ascetic ideal of voluntary poverty amongst monks, nuns and friars,

---

[57] Brian Griffiths concludes his argument in this way, pp.178-9:
'The Christian faith affirms the right to private ownership, the freedom to do business in the market place and the rule of law. These are basic institutions of global capitalism and the foundation of economic freedom, something that is valuable in itself. They provide the basis for innovation and creativity and along with trade and cross-border investment, they are a source for the growth of prosperity and the reduction of poverty in developing countries. It is inconceivable that global poverty could be eliminated without the private sector playing a major role. The appeal by Christians to economic justice must embrace wealth creation as well as wealth distribution.
    Second, to support the key institutions of global capitalism is not to advocate *laissez-faire* economics or to subscribe to a libertarian philosophy. Within a Christian perspective, free markets must be set within a framework of laws and regulations which aim to ensure fairness and justice, and be anchored in the values of integrity and trust which respects the dignity of each individual.
    Third, global corporations are at the heart of global capitalism and the process of globalization. In the way they do business, global corporations express certain values. They should be encouraged to develop core values, to set out these values explicitly and then to be held accountable for them. By taking the initiative to act responsibly, the business community will prevent unnecessary and cumbersome legislation by governments or supra-governmental bodies, which would simply impose higher costs on companies and disincentives for their investment in developing countries.
    Fourth, global capitalism needs global governance, but not global government. Global capitalism is a process which must be managed and global governance improved in the interest of fairness ...
    Fifth, the global market economy has its limitations. Following the example of Christ, the Christian will identify in a special way with the poor, the hungry, the excluded. Unless specific initiatives are taken by NGOs, governments, and international institutions, the extremely poor of the world will remain barely touched by global capitalism. The Christian church worldwide, which historically has been a major source of voluntary and charitable initiatives, is still committed to the task of serving the needy. More than ever global capitalism is challenging the church to face the full implications of its calling.'

[58] Sallie McFague, in *Subverting Greed*, p.119:
Herman E Daly and John B Cobb in *For the Common Good*, Beacon Press Boson, 2nd Edition 1994, P. 405 who emphasise that economic activity should serve the community and who advocate a Christian bio-centrism, are also very critical of much Christian teaching. 'Christian theism has done much to bring about the dangerous situation to which the world has come. In varied forms it has supported anthropocentrism, ignored or belittled the natural world, opposed efforts to stop population growth, directed attention away from the urgent needs of this life, treated as absolute authority for today teachings that were meant to influence a very different world, aroused false hopes, given false assurances, and claimed God's authority for all these sins.'

who followed the same path, has made an important contribution to Christian living, (although) this is not the way required of all Christians".[59] They also would agree with John Taylor's little book, *Enough is Enough*, which was quite influential in the seventies in church circles in Britain.

Enough is enough

Taylor began by drawing attention to *The Limits of Growth*, which was written in 1972 by Dennis L Meadows and his colleagues at the Massachusetts Institute of Technology. The conclusions of the study were deeply pessimistic.

> If the global figures for population growth and for industrial output continue to rise ... then the natural resources which are non-renewable will become exhausted during the next century. If that model is corrected by new discoveries of non-renewable resources and by recycling wherever possible, then a rising pollution of the environment will bring about a drastic decline in food production early in the next century.
>
> If besides solving the problem of natural resources, pollution is statutorily reduced, then industrial production can have a longer lease of life, but the population explosion will exhaust food supplies.
>
> Even if the population is leveled off and the research enables us to double our food yields, then the exhaustion of the land, the eventual depletion of resources and the slower but still inexorable accumulation of pollution must ensure the collapse of the human life-system by the end of the next century.[60]

The report did suggest that it was not too late to change the life-style of the West, but as John Taylor observed:

---

59 Trevor Shannon in *Ethical Issues in Six Religions*, ed. Peggy Morgan and Clive Lawton, Edinburgh University Press, 1996, p.191.
60   John V Taylor, *Enough is Enough*, p.3, referring to Donella H. Meadows, Dennis L Meadows. Jorgen Randers, William W. Behrens III, *The Limits to Growth*, Earth Island Ltd, 1972.

> There is no surer way of arousing the
> emotions of economists than to suggest that
> the highly developed countries of the West
> should deliberately stop the growth of
> capital investment, slow down industry's
> consumption of raw materials and set about
> educating the citizens to expect a leveling-
> off of the standards of living ...[61]

Both the facts and the arguments were challenged. John Taylor
recognized this. He called for more research but also suggested that:

> In the meantime what everyone of us can do
> is to forgo the lethal folly of our ways and
> then to throw our whole weight into a
> sustained campaign against the attitudes of
> our affluent society and all those who
> deliberately seek to engender them in us ...
> It is intolerable to maintain the ever-rising
> standards of the few upon the poverty of the
> many ... The rich – ourselves – must learn
> to be content with less. That means that as
> import prices go up, wages, salaries,
> dividends, rents and tariffs do not, and we
> find humane ways of spreading the loss and
> finding new avenues of employment. Excess
> is the subject of this book and the enemy I
> shall try to invite you to fight year in and
> year out.[62]

---

61 John V Taylor, *Enough is Enough*, pp.52-3.
62 John V Taylor, *Enough is Enough*, p.21.

John Taylor did this with superb pulpit oratory. The significance of John Taylor's book is that he develops the "theology of enough". The Hebrew dream, he says, was summed up in the word *shalom*, "The harmony of a caring community informed at every point by its awareness of God".[63] Such harmony was endangered by excessive covetousness (*betsa*).[64] The emphasis is on co-operation rather than competition. Work is a person's contribution to the good of society. For this certainly a person should get a proper reward, but what we can give to the community is more valuable than what we get out of it.

The warning note sounded in the report *The Limits to Growth*, which Taylor quoted, is echoed in *Threshold 2000*, which was prepared by the Millennium Institute for the 1999 Parliament of the World's Religions, which was held in Cape Town. The overview begins with these words:

> If the present beliefs and policies continue, the world in the twenty-first century will be more crowded, more polluted, less stable economically and ecologically, and more vulnerable to violent disruption than the world we live in now. Serious stresses involving inter-religious relations, the economy, population, resources, environment, and security loom ahead. Overall, Earth's people will be poorer in many ways than they are today.

---

63 John V Taylor, *Enough is Enough*, p.41.
64 The horror of voracious greed was vividly expressed in the Book of Proverbs:

> *The leech has two daughters;*
> *'Give', says one and 'give' says the other.*
> *Three things there are which will never be satisfied.*
> *Four which never say 'Enough!'*
> *The grave and a barren womb,*
> *A land thirsty for water*
> *And fire that never says 'Enough.'*

The New Testament frequently condemns "covetousness" or "ruthless greed", as the New English Bible translates the Greek word *pleonexia*.

> For more than a billion of Earth's desperately
> poor humans, the outlook for food and
> other necessities of life will be no better. For
> many it will be worse.[65]

The main author of the report was Gerald Barney, who gave a similar doom laden keynote address to the 1993 Parliament of the World's Religions in Chicago. In describing the task ahead, Gerald Barney's emphasis is on the need for a mutually enhancing relationship between humans and the Earth. "Nations are not independent entities subject to no other power on Earth. They are all interdependent and very much subject to the health and welfare of the entire ecosystem of Earth".[66] Parents, he insisted, should teach their children "the difference between needs and wants and the meaning of enough".[67]

The environmental question is so important that it requires a chapter to itself. I want here to focus on the emphasis on "enough" to be found in both John V Taylor and Gerald Barney's writings. Their warnings about excess and greed are important, but is wealth creation necessarily a form of greed? What is the dividing line between excess and proper provision for one's family? I wonder, also, whether a slow down of consumption in the developed world would in fact benefit people in poorer countries or lead to a recession that might do more harm than good? Is there a way in which such a slow down could be managed so that it reduced the economic injustices in our world? I recall quoting with approval the slogan "Live simply, so that others may simply live", but is it as simple as that? John Taylor himself quotes the American economist James Weaver, who said, "If all of us decided that our homes were adequate, our cars satisfactory, our clothing sufficient, our present sort of economics would collapse tomorrow. For it is built

---

65 Gerald O Barney, *Threshold 2000, Critical Issues and Spiritual Values for a Global Age,* CoNexus Press 1999, p.17.
66 Gerald O Barney, *Threshold 2000, Critical Issues and Spiritual Values for a Global Age,* p.87.
67 Gerald O Barney, *Threshold 2000, Critical Issues and Spiritual Values for a Global Age,* p.89.

on the assumption that man's wants are insatiable".[68] We need economists to offer alternative models that make sustainable development and the relief of poverty the priorities.

Some Western economists, such as E F Schumacher, have hoped to find an answer in Buddhism.

Buddhism

Renunciation and a simple life style are highly regarded in Buddhism and Hinduism. Taylor refers to the influential book *Small is Beautiful* by E F Schumacher, which commended the Buddhist ideal. Schumacher wrote:

> Buddhism is in no way antagonistic to physical well being. It is not wealth that stands in the way of liberation but attachment to wealth; not the enjoyment of pleasurable things but the craving for them. The keynote of Buddhist economics, therefore, is simplicity and non-violence. From an economist's point of view, the marvel of the Buddhist way of life is the utter rationality of its pattern – amazingly small means leading to extraordinarily satisfactory results.
>
> For the modern economist this is very difficult to understand. He is used to measuring the 'standard of living' by the amount of annual consumption, assuming all the time that a man who consumes more

---

68 Quoted by John V Taylor in *Enough is Enough*, on p.19. No reference is given..

is 'better off' that a man who consumes less. A Buddhist economist would consider this approach excessively irrational: since consumption is merely a means to human well being, the aim should be to obtain the maximum of well being with the minimum of consumption.[69]

For the Buddhist householder, wealth, honestly obtained, is a perfectly proper aim. Excess is condemned. Generosity is an important virtue and it shows that a person is not unhealthily attached to wealth and possessions. The strong monastic tradition also emphasizes the relative unimportance of material possessions.

In relation to globalization,[70] Buddhism does not separate economic (secular) issues from ethical or spiritual ones. It recognizes that no economic system is value free, and it is critical of economists who ignore the ethical and spiritual dimensions of life. Socially engaged Buddhists are working with people of other faiths to ensure that economic globalization benefits people rather than trans-national corporations.

Hinduism

In Hinduism also the pursuit of wealth and power is one of the legitimate aims of life. Indeed, the householder should actively seek wealth "because people in the other three stages of life are every day supported by the householders through the teaching of sacred

---

69 E F Schumacher, *Small is Beautiful, A Study of Economics As If People Mattered,* Abacus, 1974, p. 48.
70 David Loy, of Bunkyo University in Japan, however, gives a rather different emphasis to Buddhist teaching. Loy, referring to the story of the Lion's Roar Sutra, suggests that Buddhism encourages economic activity rather than dependence on welfare. It also recognises the state's responsibility in addressing poverty. He notes that there is not in Buddhism much talk about social or distributive justice. Instead the emphasis is on generosity, as a way in which non-attachment is cultivated and demonstrated. See David Loy's chapter in *Subverting Greed,* especially p.62 and his chapter in *Globalisation: The Perspectives and Experiences of the Religious Traditions of Asia Pacific,* eds. Joseph A.Camilleri and Chandra Muzaffar, International Movement for a Just World, 1998.

knowledge and with food, therefore, the order of the householder is the most excellent one".[71] Nevertheless, the Upanishads insist that man is not to be satisfied with wealth alone.[72] Indeed, when the householder grows old and sees wrinkles in his skin and grayness in his hair, he should relinquish his responsibilities and with his wife retire to the forest. Indeed, there is a prevailing spirit of renunciation and the *sannyasi,* who abandons worldly possessions is much admired as the ideal man. India, has nevertheless seen rapid industrial and business expansion.

Hindus recognize that the ill effects of greed are just as apparent at the international level. National governments and international organizations need to be powerful enough to ensure that economic activity is for the benefit of the whole community. "The religious mission", writes, Swami Agnivesh, who is chair of the UN Trust Fund on Contemporary Forms of Slavery, "is to enunciate and popularize a counter-culture to the emerging and reigning culture of consumerism and indulgence".[73]

Common themes

Between the extremes of unbridled capitalism and total renunciation, most religions, despite varieties of emphasis, seem to agree on the importance of wealth creation and the relief of poverty. They recognize that human beings need material resources to live a fulfilling life. The provision of such resources is an honorable and worthy activity. Work should be seen as a contribution to the good of the community. If, however, the primary purpose of economic activity is the accumulation of wealth rather than meeting a legitimate need, it has become distorted. Religions insist that greed undermines society and diverts

---

71 Manusmriti 3, 78.
72 Katha Upanishad 1, 1. 27; Brihadaranyaka Upanishad 4, 3, 33ff.
73 Swami Agnivesh, *Subverting Greed,* p.48.

human beings from true personal fulfillment. Greed is not only a danger to our spiritual life, it impoverishes others and threatens the environment. As Frank Buchman, founder of Moral Re-Armament said, "There is enough in the world for everyone's need, but not for everyone's greed".[74]

I do not wish to hide the real differences of emphasis between and within some religions, but there is, I believe, enough common ground for faith communities to unite in questioning the ideology of greed that so often fuels economic globalization as we know it. Religions emphasize co-operation rather than competition.

It is recognized that there should be no dishonesty nor exploitation of workers and of the poor. A proportion of wealth should be devoted to the relief of poverty – God's special concern for the poor is often stressed. It is now widely acknowledged that there should be no exploitation of the environment – a concern especially emphasized in Jainism and in Native Spirituality.

Moreover, members of faith communities should together support campaigns for debt relief, fairer trade, a more just distribution of wealth and the protection of the environment and work for the strengthening of civil society.

An even greater responsibility, however, is to hold aloft a vision of the God-given dignity and value of each person, which is totally independent of his or her achievements. Without this vision the distinctive contribution that the faiths can bring to particular campaigns will be lost. This vision derives not just from the moral teaching of the faiths, but from their core spiritual experience, which both unites us with Ultimate Reality and also unites us in sympathy with all people and all life.

In the next chapter we shall see how the vision and the values that religions share can help to transform global economic activity so that it becomes genuinely co-operative and serves the good of all people.

---

74 Frank Buchman, *Remaking the World*, 1947, p.56.

A NEW ECONOMY NEEDS
A NEW MORALITY

A New Economy needs
a New Morality

A moral vacuum[1]

"A New Economy needs a new morality … there's a moral vacuum at the heart of the New Economy that needs to be filled". Not a quote from a sermon but from *Business Week's* chief economist.[2] The guru of the World Economic Forum, George Soros, has said the same. A purely transactional approach to economic activity governed by the principle of self-interest, which he labels "market fundamentalism", is in danger of undermining social values and loosening moral constraints.[3]

Law cannot itself create an atmosphere of trust that is necessary for honest business dealings. The emphasis on accountability and assessment is itself partly required because of a decline in personal morality. Long ago Confucius said, "Govern the people by laws and regulate them by penalties and they will try to do no wrong but they will lose the sense of shame. Govern them by virtue and restrain them by rules of propriety and the people will have a sense of shame and be reformed by themselves".[4] Truly moral behavior requires inner transformation, which is a promised goal of the various religious paths.[5]

Is this relevant to the dangers of unrestrained globalization?

---

1 Some of the material in this chapter also appears in my contribution to *Promoting the Common Good*, by Kamran Mofid and Marcus Braybrooke, Shepheard-Walwyn (Publishers), 2005.
2 Michael Mandel in *Business Week*, 25.2.02, p.115.
3 Quoted by John Dunning in *Making Globalization Good*, p. 32 referring to G. Soros, *The Crisis of Global Capitalism*, Little, Brown and Company, London, 1998, p.75.
4 Quoted by J N Behrman in *Making Globalization Good*, p. 123.
5 J N Behrman in *Making Globalization Good*, p.122.

Most religions, as I argued in the previous chapter, recognize that economic activity is beneficial provided it serves human welfare, but that greed is destructive of community life, a threat to the environment and a danger to the individual. The first task of religious thinkers, therefore, is to reclaim the moral high ground and to affirm that economic activity should conform to widely accepted moral values. It is then necessary, secondly, to spell out those moral values on which the great faiths and many people of good will agree, as has been attempted in the Parliament of World Religions' *Declaration of a Global Ethic*. Thirdly, these values need to be applied to economic activity – indeed this is beginning to happen. Fourthly, faith communities need to co-operate in a range of activities that will ensure that economic development benefits the poor – especially the very poor - as much as the rich. Above all, there is need to ensure that education at every level gives due attention to moral concerns.

A moral framework

Jonathan Sacks, as we have seen, takes an essentially positive view of globalization. He argues strongly, however, "that the markets depend on virtues not created by the state".[6] "There is no way of bypassing difficult moral choices by way of scientific decision-procedure that states: 'Maximize X'. We first have to decide which X we wish to maximize, and how to weigh X against Y when the pursuit of one damages the fulfillment of the other. The human project is inescapably a moral project ... The ultimate value we should be concerned to maximize is human dignity – the dignity of all human beings, equally, as children of the creative, redeeming God".[7]

Sacks illustrates this by suggesting that a visitor to London, having seen the Houses of Parliament and the Stock Exchange, might

---

6 J. Sacks, *The Dignity of Difference*, p.152.
7 J. Sacks in *Making Globalization Good*, pp. 228-9.

come to St Paul's Cathedral. There the visitor might ask, "What do houses of worship create and distribute?" Jonathan Sacks's answer is that congregations do create and distribute something, but it is significantly different from power and wealth. "Political and economic relationships are *contractual*. They presuppose the coming together of self-interested parties, both of whom benefit from the exchange ... Contractual relationships, however, are not the only or even the most fundamental forms of association". Dr Sacks then points to family life which should reflect certain fundamental concepts such as "love, loyalty, responsibility, authority, obedience, fairness and compassion".[8] Families illustrate what Sacks calls "*covenantal* relationships". These, he suggests, are essential to a healthy society. [9]

George Soros, as Sacks notes, has also said that financiers today depend not on trust but on the presence of lawyers, because business does not now depend on long-term relationships but has become transactional, or a series of one-off encounters. As a result, Soros warns, "when expediency becomes established as the social norm, society become unstable".[10] Sacks summarizes his argument by saying, "The state depends on virtues not created by the state".[11] He goes on to say that:

> One of the classic roles of religion has been
> to preserve a space – physical and
> metaphysical – immune to the pressures of

---

8 J. Sacks, *The Dignity of Difference*, p.149.

9 Sacks quotes Francis Fukuyama, who has written:
"If the institutions of democracy and capitalism are to work properly, they must coexist with certain pre-modern cultural habits that ensure their proper functioning. Law, contract, and economic rationality provide a necessary but not sufficient basis for both the stability and the prosperity of post-industrial societies; they must be as well leavened with reciprocity, moral obligations, duty toward the community, and trust, which are based in habit rather than rational calculation. The latter are not anachronisms in a modern society but rather the *sine qua non* of the latter's success.'"
Francis Fukuyama, *Trust*, Hamish Hamilton, London, 1995, p. 11 quoted by Sacks, *Dignity of Difference*, p.152.

10 George Soros, *The Crisis of Global Capitalism*, p.80.

11 Sacks, *The Dignity of Difference*, p.152.

the market. When we stand before God we
do so regardless of what we earn, what we
own, what we buy, what we can afford. We
do as beings of ultimate non-transactional
value, here because someone – some force at
the heart of being – called us into existence
and summoned us to be a blessing ... (The
great religions) value people for what they
are.[12]

The Archbishop of Canterbury, Dr Rowan Williams, seemed
to reach a similar conclusion towards the end of his Dimbleby Lecture,
which provoked widespread discussion. Much of William's argument
was about the nation state being replaced by the market state. The
danger of this, he said, is that human beings are seen as commodities.
"Because of its abandonment of a clear morality for the public sphere,
the market state is in danger of linking its legitimacy, its right to be
taken seriously by citizens, to its capacity to maximize varieties of
personal insurance".[13] He suggests that religious communities may be
able to fill the moral vacuum by providing a place where the human
being is valued as a unique individual:

The sheer presence of the church – or any
place of religious activity in the middle of
communities of primary deprivation ...
indicates that there is still a place where you
can give voice to other accounts of
humanity. The historic role of the Church
of England has been and still is to make
such space available ... witnessing to certain

---

12   Sacks, *The Dignity of Difference*, p. 158.
13   Rowan Williams, *The Dimbleby Lecture*, 19.12.02 www.timesonline.co.uk/article/0,343

non-negotiable things about humanity and
the context in which humanity lives.[14]

Earlier Dr Williams had said:

> For the religious believer ... each of us, and
> each item in our environment, exists first in
> relation to something other than me, my
> needs, my instincts. They are related to a life
> or agency quite independent of any aspect
> of how things happen to be or happen to
> turn out in the universe; to the eternal, to
> God.[15]

Both Dr Sacks and Dr Williams speak of the role of the faith
communities in making or preserving a space in which the human being
is recognized to have inherent worth.

Many people of faith see the sacredness of life as grounded in
the divine origins of the universe. For example, Theists claim that every
human life is valuable in its own right, because every person is "a child
of God". Societies that do not speak of God may refer to an "Original
Source of Law".[16] Religions share a conviction that this is a moral
universe, whether they teach that all people will be accountable for their
actions at a Last Judgment or that all people are subject to the law of
karma, by which they reap the fruits of their behavior. There are, of
course, many people who do not believe in a Transcendent Reality who
are committed to human rights and the sacredness of life, but, as C S
Lewis claimed, all the great religious leaders and philosophers
throughout history have believed in the concept of absolute values and
that certain moral attributes are really true and that others are false.[17]

---

14 *Ibid*, p. 15.
15 *Ibid*, p. 13.
16 J N Berhamn in *Making Globlization Good*, p.116.
17 J Dunning in *Making Globalization Good*, p. 355 referring to C S Lewis, *The Abolition of Man*,
Collins 1978. No page given.

There is in the teaching of the great religions, striking agreement about what these values are. Each religion and society has its particular ethical code of behavior, but behind the variety, agreed principles can be discerned and recently, several attempts have been made to spell out what is often called "a Global Ethic".

A global ethic

Many spiritual leaders now recognize the need for a Global Ethic. Muslims, Buddhists, Jews, Hindus, Jains and others as well as Christians have said "Yes" to a Global Ethic.[18] Let Pope John Paul II serve as an example. In 2001, he said, "As humanity embarks upon the process of globalization, it can no longer do without a common code of ethics". He added, "This does not mean a single dominant socio-economic system or culture which would impose its values and its criteria on ethical reasoning. It is within man as such, within universal humanity sprung from the Creator's hand, that the norms of social life are to be sought. Such a search is indispensable if globalization is not to be just another name for the absolute relativization of values and the homogenization of lifestyles and cultures. In all the variety of cultural forms, universal human values exist and they must be brought out and emphasized as the guiding force of all development and progress". [19]

The best known, but not the only effort to produce a Global Ethic is the Declaration that was signed by most members of the 1993 Assembly of the Parliament of the World's Religions and for which much preparatory work had been done by Professor Hans Küng.[20] Based on the fundamental demand that every human being must be treated humanely, the Declaration affirms four "Irrevocable Directives":

---

18 See *Yes to a Global Ethic,* ed. Hans Küng, SCM Press 1996.
19 Pope John Paul II in an Address to the Papal Academy of Social Sciences on 27.4.01. Vatican website.
20 See, *Stepping Stones to a Global Ethic,* ed Marcus Braybrooke, SCM Press 1992 and *For All Life,* ed. Leonard Swidler, White Cloud Press, Ashland, Oregon 1999.

Commitment to a culture of non-violence and respect for life.
Commitment to a culture of solidarity and a just economic order.
Commitment to a culture of tolerance and a life of truthfulness.
Commitment to a culture of equal rights and partnership between men and women.

The global ethic is not intended to be a substitute for the specific moral teaching of particular religions. Hans Küng himself says, "The global ethic is no substitute for the Torah, the Gospels, the Qur'an, the Bhagavad Gita, the Discourses of the Buddha or the Teachings of Confucius and other scriptures". It is concerned simply with a "minimal basic consensus relating to binding values, irrevocable standards and moral attitudes which can be affirmed by all religions despite their dogmatic differences and can also be supported by non-believers". [21]

Certainly the ethical element in a religion has to be understood in the context of the whole. "The source of vision and motivation for people of religious belief is their experience of the supreme reality, the transcendent, or the divine".[22] Moral concern cannot be separated from inner transformation, but as twentieth-century religious leaders of several traditions have insisted, such inner transformation also embraces a concern for the well-being of the whole society. Mahatma Gandhi said, "The only way to find God is to see him in his creation and to be one with it. This can only be done by service of all, *sarvodaya*".[23]

Although for most believers their ethical conduct is part of their whole faith commitment, I believe it is possible, as the Global Ethic attempts to do, to see fundamental commonalities. Indeed, the Golden Rule is to be found in almost all religious traditions. In the same way, as I argued in the introduction to *Stepping Stones to a Global Ethic*, the

---

21 Hans Küng, *A Global Ethic for Global Politics and Economics,* SCM Press 1997, *p.*109
22 See *Millennium Challenges for Development and Faith Institutions*, The World Bank, 2003.
23 Mahatma Gandi, *Harijan.*

contemporary concern for human rights, even if expressed in the thought forms of the Enlightenment, is grounded in faith traditions.[24]

It may be that attempts to articulate universal human rights and to identify a global ethic have been too much expressed in Western thought forms. Yet this does not invalidate the effort, but indicates that wider participation is necessary to improve these efforts. Both the books *For All Life*, which Leonard Swidler edited, and *Testing the Global Ethic*, which Peggy Morgan and I edited, include comments on the Global Ethic from members of several world religions. The task, as Leonard Swidler makes clear, is not complete. "But", he writes, "when the *Universal Declaration of a Global Ethic* is finally drafted – after multiple consultation, revision and eventual acceptance by the full range of religious and ethical institutions – it will serve as a minimal ethical standard for humankind to live up to, much as the United Nation's 1948 *Universal Declaration of Human Rights* has done. Through the former, the moral force of the world's religions and ethical institutions can be brought to bear especially on those issues which are not susceptible to the legal and political force of the latter".[25]

A practical agenda

Generalized moral exhortation can easily be ignored. On the basis of the *Global Ethic*, it is now vital for people of faith to focus attention on specific issues. This is beginning to happen, but there is a need for more interfaith discussion of specific issues. Let me give two examples of attempts to do this – first by Rabbi Dr Norman Solomon and secondly by Dr Brian Griffiths.

---

24 Louis Henken said that "all major religions proudly lay claim to fathering human rights." Louis Henken, *The Rights of Man Today*, Westview Press, 1978, p.xii. Likewise, Section 4 of the report, *Poverty and Development*, says that "the present articulation of human rights is a secular formation of the spiritual notion of the dignity inherent to each person, and thus has its grounding in the basic principles of all religions."
25 *For All Life*, ed Leonard Swidler, p.18.

First, Rabbi Dr Norman Solomon has shown clearly how ancient injunctions in the Biblical book of Leviticus can have a contemporary application to a globalized economy. For example:

> Provide credit for those who need it, but not in such a way that they cannot discharge their debts (no interest): *Global extension – international finance, favourable terms.*
>
> Provide opportunity for remission of excessive debt (sabbatical release): *Global extension – rescheduling and remission of debt.*
> Do not over-exploit the land (let it 'rest' every seven years):   *Global extension – conserve the environment.*[26]

Secondly, Brian Griffiths, writing as a Christian, identifies three key issues. *The first is the gross inequalities in our world and the plight of the extremely poor.* Of a world population of 6.1 billion people, the richest *one* per cent has as much income as the poorest *fifty-seven* per cent. This is abhorrent. In developing countries that have been drawn into the orbit of globalization, living standards have improved, but the very poor have hardly been touched by globalization. Indeed the poorest nations instead of receiving any benefit from globalization, have seen incomes falling and poverty rising. In sub-Saharan Africa, during the nineteen nineties, the number of people who were undernourished doubled from 89 million to 180 million. Such poverty is degrading, it diminishes human dignity and is a denial of the sacredness of human life, which, as we have seen, is a tenet of almost every religion.

Although Griffiths, as we have seen, argues that Christians should support global capitalism,[27] he recognizes that a redistribution of

---

26 Norman Solomon in *Subverting Greed*, p 115.
27 This includes the privitization of state-owned industries, the opening up of economies to trade and investment and allowing competitive markets to grow. See note 57 of chapter 4.

resources is needed "to help the developing world adjust to the enormous changes that opening up their economies to globalization requires". This involves debt relief and focused assistance with basic infrastructure, such as roads, electricity and telecommunications. In some countries, the poor are handicapped by lack of property rights and poor access to credit. This can be changed. In addition, Griffiths acknowledges the churches' past contribution in terms of providing schools and hospitals and emphasizes the role that charities can play in helping the very poor to build a better life for themselves and their families.

The second issue which Griffiths emphasizes is the injustice of present patterns of world trade. International trade is worth $10 million a minute, but poor countries only account for 0.4% of this trade. According to the UN, rigged trade rules cost the developing world $700 billion a year.[28] A glaring example of this is the subsidized export of food to poorer countries. The European Union and the United States currently spend $360 billion on this compared to the $53.7 dollars that they spend on overseas aid. The imports of cheap food have had devastating affects on the agricultural economies of developing countries, which have been forced to reduce protection for their own producers.

Sugar is one example. The world sugar market is chronically over-supplied. Even so the European Union, which imposes high tariffs on imported sugar, produces far more sugar than it needs. The surplus is dumped at prices well below the cost of production in countries in the Caribbean or in Mozambique. This has a devastating effect on sugar producers in such countries and is costly for citizens of the EU. At present the EU spends about 3 billion euros on export subsidies for sugar – that is, 3.30 euros for each 1 euro-worth of sugar that is exported.[29]

---

28 Figures from Christian Aid's Trade Justice Campaign.
29 Further information from the Fairtrade Foundation, www.fairtrade.org.uk; Traidcraft, www.traidcraft.co.uk; CAFOD, www.cafod.org.uk; Christian Aid, www.christianaidconnect.org.

Local producers cannot compete with this heavily subsidized sugar. David Dlamini had been growing sugar cane in South Africa for 27 years, but last year he gave up farming because he could no longer make ends meet. "You worked for months and when you looked at your expenses, you found you never covered your costs," said this father of seven children. Now the sugar cane stands rotting in his fields north of Durban.[30] Religious development charities have been highlighting the iniquity of present trade patterns for some time. As I write, the World Trade Organisation seems to have reached a much delayed agreement, which Supachai Panitchpakdi, Director General of the World Trade Organisation described as "truly historic", to address this problem. It is claimed that the agreement will boost the economy by $500 billion.[31] One waits to see if it will be implemented. The urgency of this issue was made clear by Gordon Brown, British Chancellor of the Exchequer, when he wrote:

> With three-quarters of the world's poor living in rural areas, opening up agricultural markets offers the best and quickest route for reducing poverty. Subsides to agriculture which run at one billion dollars a day – six times the amount spent on development assistance – are in urgent need of reform.[32]

Equally unjust is the way pharmaceutical companies from rich countries have patented natural resources, such as indigenous plants used for medicinal purposes, without paying any royalties to the country from which they are taken. Moreover, these companies have often denied developing countries access to new science and technology and charged excessive prices for drugs – as has been the case with the drugs needed for the treatment of HIV/Aids in Africa.

---

30 Information from CAFOD.
31 Report by Edmund Conway in *The Daily Telegraph*, 2.8.04.
32 Gordon Brown, in *Tackling Poverty: A Global New Deal*, HM Treasury, 2002, quoted by Brian Griffiths in *Making Globalization Good*, p. 175.

Pharmaceutical firms make their money from selling products to the customers in rich nations. As a result, the focus of research is biased against the poor. Médécins Sans Frontières reckons that between 1975 and 1997, out of 1,223 new medicines brought to the market, only thirteen were for the treatment of tropical diseases, which are prevalent in poor countries. Moreover, wealthy nations attract doctors and nurses from developing countries, depriving their people of basic health care.

Protection of the environment is the third issue, which Griffiths identifies and to which we shall turn our attention in the next chapter. He writes, "At the heart of this concern is a moral issue. It is simply not possible for science, ecology, or economics to find a reason for subscribing to a concept such as sustainable development. One is forced to turn to ethics or religion".[33]

It is instructive to compare the three key issues identified by Griffiths with the four building blocks for a global new deal, highlighted by Gordon Brown. These are:

Improvement in the terms on which the poorest countries participate in the global economy.

Adoption by international business companies of high corporate standards.

An improved trade regime so that developing countries participate on fair terms in the world economy.

Substantial transfer of additional resources from the richest to the poorest countries in the form of investment for development.

The fourth issue is one on which people of faith have long campaigned. For example, in the nineteen sixties I helped form a World Development Movement group in the Medway towns in Kent. Recently, the European Union has agreed to increase its contribution to development assistance, as has the United States.

---

33 Brian Griffiths, *Making Globalization Good*, p. 175.

A voice for the poor

All this highlights one way in which people of faith can speak for the poor. In fact it is a double task: to inform the general public of the issues and to create a popular demand for action and to bring pressure on governments. The two go together. Governments are reluctant to act without public support but they also need to be challenged to meet their commitments.

One striking example of a faith-based campaign is the Jubilee 2000 Debt campaign. This linked debt relief to the Biblical concept of Jubilee and to the new millennium. In the book of Leviticus the idea of the Sabbath is extended to a seventh or Sabbath year in which the land is left fallow. In the forty-ninth year, there is a complete redistribution of wealth including the cancellation of debts and the freeing of slaves.[34] Jubilee affiliates campaigned in more than 60 countries and gained support in many faith communities. The World Bank was already concerned about the serious damage caused to development by debt, but Jubilee 2000 brought the issue to public attention, as James D Wolfensohn, President of the World Bank acknowledged.[35]

Another example of faith communities influencing political and economic decision-making is the way how The World Faiths Development Dialogue (WFDD) has helped the World Bank to expand its understanding of poverty. At the first meeting of faith leaders with representatives of the World Bank, the meaning of poverty was discussed. Subsequently, the World Faiths Development Dialogue held further consultations with faith representatives and also worked on the Poverty Reduction Strategy Paper (PRSP) process, which included a survey of some 60,000 people in poor communities across the world.

---

34 Leviticus,chapter 25.
35 In a speech on 6.4.2000. Quoted in *Mind, Heart and Soul, in the Fight Against Poverty,* ed Katherine Marshall and Lucy Keough, The World Bank, 2004, p.35.

The intention is that development strategies while making economic sense are also compatible with the hopes and the aspirations of a country's people. Faith participants have made clear that they see poverty as a complex phenomenon. They give more attention to freedom and a satisfying life than to gains in income or improvements in social indicators.

Practical involvement of people of faith

It is in local projects on the ground that faith communities have a special influence. They often possess unrivalled local knowledge, have the respect of the people and a network of communication. Let me give two examples: the efforts of Tostan in Senegal to stop female genital cutting, and the role of faith-based groups in Uganda in combating "Slim" (HIV/AIDS). It is estimated that female genital cutting, which is sometimes called *kene-kene* or *khitan* has been practiced on some 130 million women or girls alive today. An additional 2 million are at risk of undergoing this procedure every year. It is a practice condemned by numerous international conventions.

In Senegal's Thiès region a Non-governmental organization called Tostan has for many years tried to educate people to stop this practice. In July 1996 it received help from the American Jewish Women's Committee to produce non-formal educational modules. By September 1996, the women of the village of Malicounda Bambara decided they wanted to end the practice of female genital cutting. From October 1996 to May 1997, the women led a campaign to end the practice, beginning with their husbands and extending it to religious leaders, other women, and the village chief. In June 1997, Tostan staff discovered that there had been no cutting in the village during that year and at the end of July, twenty Sengalese journalists came to Malicounda Bambara to hear the women there make a public declaration to end female genital cutting in their village. Soon afterwards, Imam Demba

Diawara was invited to hear the women's testimony about the harmful effects of cutting – a subject which had been virtually taboo. The imam was shaken by what the women said and impressed by their determination to end it. As a first step he walked to ten neighboring villages to discuss with religious and traditional leaders the need to put an end to cutting. In February 1998, eight months after the Malicounda Bambar declaration, leaders of thirteen villages in the Thiès region issued the Diabougou Declaration publicly committing them to end the practice. By late 1998, religious leaders throughout Senegal had begun to support its elimination and in 1999, the Senegalese Parliament passed a law officially abolishing female genital cutting. In early 2004, it was estimated that over one thousand communities have abandoned the practice after taking part in Tostan educational programs. [36]

In Uganda, the popular name for HIV/AIDS is "Slim", because of the emaciating effect the disease has on its victims. In 1986 President Museveni established the National Commission for the Prevention of AIDS in collaboration with the World Health Organisation. Because religion is "inextricably woven into every aspect of life in Uganda", it was important to involve religious leaders. Uganda's HIV/AIDS program, which is sensitive to religious concerns, is based on ABC: '"Practice Abstinence, Be faithful and Use Condoms". Catholic, Protestant and Muslim leaders have actively participated in the work of the Commission, and have played a central role in efforts to combat Slim. "In the epidemic's early years, when the government focused on prevention, faith-based health services recognized that patient care and counseling were woefully neglected. In the intervening years, faith based groups and a host of volunteers, many trained and administered by religious organizations, have provided counseling, home based care, provision for orphans and increasingly drug therapy." It is reckoned that more than half of the two thousand NGOs engaged in HIV/AIDS initiatives are faith based. [37]

---

36 *Mind, Heart and Soul,* pp. 159-162.
37 *Mind, Heart and Soul,* p.105-123.

Ethics in business and public life

But I come back to the need for moral values. There are many pressing issues on which action needs to be taken, but the moral will is lacking. This is why, as I have said, faith communities should engage in educating the public. But effective improvements in the living standards of the poor are seriously threatened by corruption and dishonesty in governments and business. The need for ethical practices is recognized by some government and business leaders and there is some welcome progress in putting this into effect, but such values can only in part be enforced by regulation. It requires also the inner motivation of those who take part in public and business life – especially of those in leadership positions as their example for good or ill influences others.

Corruption is a serious drain on the economies of some countries and a disincentive to investment. For several years, Transparency International has sought to address this and a major International Anti-Corruption Conference is held each year. Democracies are usually less corrupt and have seldom initiated war against other nations. As Winston Churchill said, "No one pretends that democracy is perfect or all-wise. Indeed, it has been said that democracy is the worst form of Government except all those other forms that have been tried from time to time".[38] In many countries public confidence in the honesty of governments is dangerously low. Many people in the US and Britain have felt they were misled, whether or not deliberately, about the supposed Weapons of Mass Destruction in Iraq. They now question whether warnings of terrorist activity are genuine or for political reasons. They also feel that the electoral system is manipulated by the wealthy and powerful. This can lead to a dangerous disillusionment, with many people opting out of political life and not bothering to vote – thus opening the door for extremists.

---

38 Winston Churchill, *Hansard*, 11.11.1947, col 206.

Transparency and accountability of government is very important, as also is a strong civil society.

The need for higher ethical standards in financial and business life have been highlighted by the Enron scandal and the discovery that the banking system underpinned financial transfers by terrorists involved in the 11th of September attacks. There has, therefore, been an effort to a clamp down on money laundering. Robert Davies, Chief Executive of the Prince of Wales International Business Leaders' Forum, suggests, "There is clear evidence of shifting public attitudes on a global scale and in the media against short-term irresponsible behavior of companies, and in particular trans-national companies and those with high profile brands".[39]

Various codes of business behavior have been produced and a growing number of firms are adopting their own ethical guidelines. Some examples are the Ethics Program launched by the Inter-American Development Bank, the "Interfaith Declaration: A Code of Ethics on International Business for Christians, Muslims and Jews" and the "Principles for Business" of the Caux Round Table.[40] The latter two statements agree that companies have responsibilities over and above earning profits. Maximizing profit should not be the sole motive of economic activity. Shareholders, it is suggested, should see themselves as stakeholders with a responsibility for all who have a stake in a business. Companies should recognize that they have a responsibility to their employees, to customers, to suppliers and financiers and to the community, and also to owners, shareholders or investors. Some companies recognize their environmental responsibilities and have an environmental audit.

An ethical approach to business is having some effect. The Institute of Business Ethics (IBE) was established in 1986. Its latest

39 Robert Davies in *Making Globalization Good*, p. 310.
40 See further Hans Küng, *A Global Ethic for Global Politics and Economics*, SCM Press 1997, especially pp.251-4.

survey shows that a growing number of companies now provide a code
of ethics for their employees and are also showing an interest in
ethical/social audits – although too often these codes are not translated
into other languages for local use. A major concern is the source of
supplies, especially if child labor is involved or working conditions are
unacceptable. The Institute gives some examples of good practice. One
is that Nestlé – rightly criticized for promoting baby milk in Africa –
has in Russia sponsored the TV version of the popular children's show
Sesame Street to make children aware of the link between diet and
health. The Prince of Wales Business Leaders Forum (PWBLF), set up
in 1990, aims "to promote responsible business practices
internationally that benefit business and society, and which help to
achieve social, economic and environmentally sustainable development,
particularly in new and emerging market economies". Here again there
are some results. The sports footwear industry plays a large part in
Vietnam's economy. In 1997, Pentland, one of the major international
firms, commissioned a report that showed the dangers of poor
ventilation, exposure to hazardous chemicals, and inadequate safety
equipment. Subsequently, the Forum, after wide consultation, has
drawn up a communal action plan, which is now being put into effect.
In December 1998, what was said to be the first environmentally
responsible hotel was opened in Mumbai (Bombay). All the wood is
from Hevea (rubber) trees and treated to take on the properties of more
expensive woods such as teak or maple. The Hevea trees are cropped
and replanted in a 25-30 year cycle. Coat hangers are made of pressed
board obtained from recycled wood.

These are but a few examples. They help to create confidence
that those who voice ethical concerns can have an effect on industry,
both in terms of the work conditions of the labor force and in
safeguarding the environment. It is also important that businesses make
a fair return to countries whose labor and products they use. Ethical or
socially responsible investment is increasing, and shareholders are
beginning to exercise their power. Many shareholders are people of faith

and I believe with proper information far more could use their influence. But this requires faith communities to put more of their resources into the necessary research and dissemination of information.[41]

Values education

Yet morality can only to a limited extent be imposed from outside. It requires inner motivation. Long ago Plato wrote, "Education in virtue is the only education which deserves the name".[42] The importance of moral or values education at every level needs to be emphasized. This should start in the home. For a time I received copies from the USA of a magazine called *Peter's Path*, which was about "spiritual parenting". It aimed to help parents develop their children's awareness of life's spiritual dimension and a sense of values. Values education should also be part of a school's curriculum. It is widely recognized in the words of Jack Behrman, who is a Professor of International Business and Ethics, that "ethics *must* be taught – rather, learned! – and nurtured into continuing practice". Behrman complains that "the conflict over *what* values should be taught or encouraged, and the unwillingness to 'inculcate' any set pattern in 'secular' education, has caused several Western, and particularly the American, educational systems, to abandon their responsibility to teach values. But, as one sage put it, 'Teaching a student without values is to create a menace to society'".[43] Here again, the *Global Ethic*, can serve as a basis for values education, although teachers will need to relate these universal values to particular cultural and religious traditions.[44]

---

41 Robert Davies' s chapter in *Making Globalization Good*.
42 Plato, *The Laws*.
43 Jack N Behrman, *Making Globalization Good*, p.117.
44 See further *Testing the Global Ethic*, ed. Peggy Morgan and Marcus Braybrooke, World Congress of Faiths and CoNexus Press, 1998.

Questions of ethics should also underlie the different studies pursued at higher levels of education, but they are often neglected. Dr Kamran Mofid, for example, has drawn attention to the neglect of ethical issues in many university courses on economics.[45]   If that is so, it is hardly surprising that economic life has become divorced from morality.

Conclusion

If this is indeed a moral universe, as people of all faiths agree, then moral and ethical issues are relevant to the whole of life. Islam is right, in my view, to question the separation, common in Western thinking, of the secular and the sacred. It is urgent, therefore, that people of faith and those who influence political, economic and business activity join together to apply the ethical teaching of the great religions to their work.   Only by so doing will they ensure that economic activity serves the needs of all humankind rather than impoverishing and enslaving the many so that the few enjoy a wealth that most people cannot even imagine.

45 Kamran Mofid, *Globalisation for the Common Good*, Shepheard-Walwyn, 2002.

'WE ARE EARTHLINGS'

'We Are Earthlings'

The natural world is under threat

This morning, before starting to write this chapter, I glanced at *Poem for the Day*. The book fell open at Gerard Manley Hopkins' poem "God's Grandeur".

> The world is charged with the grandeur of God.
> It will flame out, like shining from shook foil;
> It gathers to a greatness, like the ooze of oil
> Crushed. Why do men then now not reck his rod?
> Generations have trod, have trod, have trod;
> And all is seared with trade; bleared, smeared with toil;
> And wears man's smudge and shares man's smell: the soil
> Is bare now, nor can foot feel, being shod.[1]

Then, as I settled at my desk, the first book I consulted began with this quotation from Leonardo da Vinci:

> All the animals languish,
> filling the air
> With lamentation.
> The woods fall in ruin.

---

[1] The sonnet "God's Grandeur", by Gerard Manly Hopkins (1844-1889), was written while Hopkins was studying theology at St Beuno's in the valley of the Elwyn in North Wales. *Poem for the Day*, is edited by Nicholas Albery, Sinclair-Stevenson, 1994, and Chatto and Windus, 2001. "God's Grandeur" is on p.168.

The mountains are torn open
In order to carry away the metals
Which are produced there.

But how can I speak of anything more wicked
than men, who with greater zeal,
have injured their country and the human race.[2]

Concern for the environment is not new, but the threats to it are now so alarming, that it has moved high on the agenda. Gerald Barney of the Millennium Institute has warned that "if present beliefs and policies continue, the world of the twenty-first century will be more crowded, more polluted, less stable economically and ecologically, and more vulnerable to violent disruption than the world we live in now". [3]

Despite many warnings, there is a reluctance to take the necessary steps to prevent ecological disaster. Although the information is available, politicians and the media cling to old patterns of thought. Problems are treated in isolation, whereas, "most of the problems faced by humanity today are interconnected and indeed have a common source".[4] There is also a sense of fatalism that "humanity is trapped in a dark fate",[5] or as Madame de Pompadour, favorite of King Louis XV of France said, "Après nous le déluge" (after us the deluge).

Can the great religions offer a compelling vision that enables people to recognize that their actions can help to preserve or devastate the environment? What we need is a new understanding that allows us to recognize that we human beings are part of a vast evolving universe.

---

2 Leonardo da Vinci, *Prophecies*, c.1490.
3 *Threshold 2000*, ed. Gerald Barney, The Millennium Institute, 2000, p.17.
4 Herman E Daly and John B Cobb, Jr, *For the Common Good*, Beacon Press, Boston, 1994 edition, p.362.
5 *For the Common Good*, p.362.

The four elements

In ancient and mediaeval cosmologies, Earth, Air, Fire and Water were regarded as fundamental constituents of the universe. These four elements are useful headings under which to outline some of the threats to the environment. There is only space to mention them almost as headlines. Even then, I do not deal with the rapid growth of population, which has seen the world's population grow in seventy-five years (roughly one lifetime) from under two billion to over six billion people.[6] I will, however, as an example, discuss problems relating to water in rather more detail. We need, at least, some awareness of the size and complexity of the problems before we look at the response of the faith communities.

Earth

Earth's thin skin of soil produces food, nurtures trees and all plant life, cleans the water, gives protection from floods and regulates the climate. Yet, globally, human beings have degraded an estimated nearly five billion acres through mismanagement, unsuitable planning, over-use of fertilizers and uncontrolled dumping of rubbish. Because of poverty many small farmers have cleared forests and cultivated fragile marginal lands, often causing soil erosion and deepening rural poverty. An estimated sixty-five per cent of Africa's agricultural land has been damaged. China has lost large areas of arable land and in North America about 235 million acres have been degraded by erosion.[7] Drylands are particularly at risk and each year some 58,000 square miles - an area larger than Greece – becomes desert. This forces inhabitants to leave their homes to search for food and work. Forests are disappearing at an

---

alarming rate and this endangers indigenous peoples and cultures as well as biodiversity. Some twenty-five acres of Earth's rainforests are destroyed every minute. Deforested soil can never again support a tropical forest or even grow crops for long, because most of the land's nutrients are in the vegetation not the soil. Deforestation can also aggravate the effects of adverse weather. In the state of Orissa in India, rapid logging of the coastal mangrove forest contributed to the terrible destruction caused by the cyclone in October 1999, which killed 7,600 people and affected nearly fifteen million people.

Air

Most people have heard of the dangers of global warming. It is said that the Earth is heating up faster than at any previous time in its history. Most reliable sources now agree that if we fail to control the emission of greenhouse gases, temperatures will rise between two to nine degrees Fahrenheit.[8] This will cause sea levels to rise, which will displace millions of people living in low-lying delta areas and lessen the amount of agricultural land available. Already, globally averaged sea level is estimated to have risen by five inches or more.[9] Deforestation has added to the problem as living trees absorb carbon dioxide. Climate change also is often a cause of "natural" disasters, while pollution can cause illness or chronic ill health.

Fire

The production of energy is a major cause of global warming. Burning fossil fuels – oil, coal and natural gas – produces carbon dioxide emissions. Reserves of oil are being used up and the need for oil can be a cause of conflict. Nuclear energy carries the risk of radiation.

The use of chemicals in industry can be hazardous, especially if

---

8 *Earth and Faith,* p.20.
9 *Celebrating Earth Holy Days,* Ed.*Susan* J Clark, Crossroad, 1992, p.31.

inadequate precautions are taken to manage and dispose of waste. The worst accident to date was at a Union Carbide plant in Bhopal in India. During the night of 2nd to 3rd December 1984, a leaky tank spewed five tons of chemicals into the air. At least 7,000 people died and half a million were made ill, some of whom suffered long term ill health and who have, still received only scant compensation.

Water

The need for clean water

Nearly twenty years ago, George Appleton, one of my spiritual teachers, said his greatest hope was that by end of the twentieth century everyone would have access to clean drinking water. Sadly, this is still far from being the case. Indeed it is predicted by the United Nations and other international organizations that the situation will get considerably worse in the next twenty-one years. It is estimated that by 2025 one third of the world's population will suffer chronic water shortages. This is partly due to added demand because of a growing world population, partly due to the adverse effects of pollution and because the greater use of water in industry and agriculture (the "green revolution"!) reduces the resources available for human consumption. If the most alarming projections for population increase occur, then nearly 7 billion people in sixty countries will face water scarcity by 2050. If the lowest population growth figures prove to be accurate, even then nearly two billion people in 48 countries will face water shortages.[10]

The vast majority (97.5%) of earth's water is salt water. Of the 2.5% of fresh water on the planet, 69% is contained in glaciers. 30% is ground water and only 0.3% is from renewable sources such as lakes and rivers. A graphic way to picture this is to imagine a gallon jug, full of water. Only one tablespoonful would be fresh water.[11]

---

10 From the *Background Briefing Book,* for the Barcelone Parliament of Religions Assembly 2004. This refers to ITT Industries Guidebook to Global Water Issues – www.itt.com/waterbook and UN2003 International Year of Fresh Water, www.wateryear2003.org.
11 From the *Background Briefing Book,* ref. Water Partners International, water.org/waterfacts.html.

Whatever the future holds, the situation is already grim. Over one billion people - 65% of whom are in Asia and 27% in Africa - are without reliable access to clean water. This means that may people drink water which has been contaminated with human and animal faecal waste which carries bacteria that can cause cholera, dysentery, typhoid fever and other waterborne diseases. Some 6,000 children die every day from diseases associated with unsafe water – this is equivalent to twenty jumbo jets crashing every day.[12] The World Health Organisation reckons that ninety per cent of these children could be saved by prevention or better treatment.

The ever present risk of illness is not the only adverse effect of lack of water. Many women and children spend long hours each day collecting water for the family. Agnes Matibya who is pump caretaker for Kashishi village in Tabora, Tanzania, explained what the situation was like when they had to walk a long way to the Taroma waterhole, before the water project in her village provided safe water in her village:

> A woman can only carry one bucket on each trip, so sometimes I had to pay 50 shillings to people who had a bicycle to get water for me. I used to get headaches and chest pains because the water was so heavy and I only used to do one trip because I was too tired. When I was pregnant, collecting water was a big problem. I had to collect it when I was nine months pregnant and I suffered; I had chest and leg pains, so I couldn't move. My stomach would hurt, so I had to stand for a while until it passed. It was hard when I gave birth because my husband had to collect water and he would only get one or

---

12 *Background Briefing Book,* ref. WHO/UNICEF Joint Monitoring Program on Water. Supply and Sanitation, Assessment 2000 Report.

two buckets, so I couldn't use much water. We had no water to drink and my husband and children would go to bed without washing.

Now I have water in the village, I am very clean; I have water to drink and I can wash my family's clothes … With the time I have free from collecting water from Taroma, I can talk and play with my children and I am happy.

As pump attendant, Agnes Matibya can also contribute to the family income. "My husband," she adds, "really appreciates and respects me now … We are really at peace now".[13]

Often it is children who have to collect water. This has several adverse effects. The heavy water pots can cause damage to the head, neck and spine. In extreme cases this may lead to deformity of the spine, which can later cause problems in pregnancy and childbirth. If mothers collect the water, older children may be left to look after their younger siblings and this may lead to accidents or younger children not being fed as regularly as they should be. Many children who collect water have to walk such a long way that they do not have time to go to school or often miss school because of illnesses caused by impure water. Yet, "Women with even a few years of basic education have smaller, healthier families, are more likely to be able to work their way out of poverty and are more likely to send their own children, girls and boys, to school. Each additional year of female education is thought to reduce child mortality by between five and ten per cent".[14]

---

13 Information from WaterAid. www.wateraid.org.uk.
14 From "Women and WaterAid'" published by WaterAid, London 2004. Ref. DFID 2000.

Lack of water ... lack of education ... higher birth rate: so many problems are interconnected. The supply of water is also linked to issues relating to globalization. Historically provision of water has been seen as a government responsibility, but the idea of water as a public good has increasingly been challenged and water is now seen as a commodity:

> In the last decade, the idea that fresh water should be increasingly subject to the rules and power of markets, prices and international trading regimes has been put into practice in dozens of ways, in hundreds of places, affecting millions of people. Prices have been set for water previously provided for free. Private corporations are taking control of the management, operation and sometimes even the ownership of previously public water systems.'[15]

As the water supply is privatized, democratic control of this basic necessity is reduced. There are now only three dominant private water industries in the world: Vivendi, Suez and Thames Water. In Europe, nine multi-national corporations now control and manage many municipal water systems and they are using the World Trade Organization to force Third World countries to grant corporate access to privatized water markets. But the water boundaries do not match up with political boundaries, so governments have limited control. Although one supposed benefit of privatization is that there would be far greater investment, in fact much investment has come from public sources like the World Bank and the International Monetary Fund and despite some successes, there have also been some spectacular failures.[16]

---

15 *Background Briefing Book*, p.25.
16 See *Just Commentary*, International Movement For a Just World, Vol. 4, No 6, June 2004, pp.1-3, and *Background Briefing Book*, pp.23-6.

Water provision not only relates to questions about globalization, but also to conflict. Scarce water supplies can be a cause of conflict, as between Israel and its neighbors, and control of water supplies can be used as a military weapon against other countries or dissidents within a country. Water supplies may also become a target for terrorists. [17]

It is often forgotten that it is not only human beings who need water. "Is all the Earth's water for humans?" Paul G Heltne, who is Co-Director of the Center for Humans and Nature, asked participants in the Barcelona Parliament of Religions. '

"Put this way" he continued, "most people quickly respond, 'Of course not. It is for all Earth's living creatures, trees and flowers, birds and mammals, amphibians and reptiles, fish, and the invertebrates. Why, no animal lives without water in some form.' Others will add that they feel that lakes and ponds, rivers and streams, glaciers and estuaries, springs and aquifers also have a right to continued existence. At this point, those responding to the question often indicate that they do so from a deeply spiritual or ethical framework".[18]

Water issues, therefore, bring to the fore the debate whether environmental concern is just a self-interested human anxiety or a recognition of the sacredness of all life. Is ecology anthropocentric or biocentric – to use the technical terms?[19]

The religious symbolism of water

Water also has profound symbolic significance in many religions. One way in which faiths can increase awareness of the environmental crisis is by exploring this symbolism and showing its contemporary relevance. This we tried to do in a "morning observance"[20] which members of the

---

17 *Background Briefing Book*, p. 24, with reference to writings by Peter Gleik of the Pacific Institute.
18 *Background Briefing Book*, p. 26.
19 See further *For the Common Good*, pp.382-89.
20 See Appendix 1.

World Congress of Faiths arranged at the Parliament of Religions. The intention was also to show that there are universal symbols that have a resonance in many faith traditions. Indeed, at several previous interfaith gatherings, people had brought water from holy rivers, such as the Jordan or the Ganges, or from sacred places, such as Zumzum. A phial of such water served as a visual focus during the observance.

The observance was in three parts. The first was a reflection on the symbolism of water in some sacred traditions. Then participants thought about the many families who do not have access to clean water, which should be the birthright of every child. Finally, participants took time to consider what they could do individually or in their own community to ensure that all people enjoy this precious gift of God and they were invited to share in a simple act of commitment.

How religions view the natural world

Although water has a symbolic or ritual importance in almost all religious traditions, the emphasis varies considerably. This is true also more widely of religions' attitude to the natural world. In recent years, religions have vied with each other to be "greener than thou". The question, therefore, is whether despite their different perspectives, they have enough in common to make together a significant impact on the contemporary environmental crisis.

God's creation

Judaism, Christianity and Islam – the three Abrahamic religions – see God's glory in nature, but insist that only the Creator is to be worshipped. Nature is not divine.

The Bible begins with the story of creation. All life is dependent on the creative and sustaining power of God. After the flood, in a covenant with Noah, God promises that "While the earth lasts seedtime and harvest, cold and heat, summer and winter, day and night, shall never cease".[21] Some twentieth-century Biblical scholars, however, have neglected this element in the Hebrew scriptures, partly because they have put their emphasis on revelation in *history* and neglected the revelation in *nature* and partly because the revelation to Moses was given at Mt Sinai in the "desert".[22]

The worship of fertility goddesses is repeatedly condemned. Nonetheless, the Psalms and the closing chapters of the book of Job rejoice in the bounty of nature and God's provision for all living beings. The Psalmist says, for example:

> *From thy high pavilion thou dost water the hills;*
> *The earth is enriched by thy provision...*
> *All of them (animals) look expectantly to thee*
> *To give them their food at the proper time;*
> *What thou givest them they gather up;*
> *When thou openest thy hand, they eat their fill.*[23]

Job is asked,

> *Do you hunt the prey for the lioness and satisfy the hunger*
> *of the lions when they crouch in their dens or lie in wait*
> *in a thicket? Who provides food for the raven when its*
> *young cry out to God*
> *and wander about for lack of food?*[24]

The bounty of nature is sometimes made conditional on Israel's obedience to the Torah. Moses warns the people:

> If you pay heed to the commandments
> which I give you this day, and love the Lord
> your God and serve him with all your heart

---

21 Genesis 8:22 (NEB).
22 See Kusumita Pedersen's chapter, "Environmental Ethics in Perspective" in *Explorations in Global Ethics: Comparative Religious Ethics and Inter-religious Dialogue,* Eds. Sumner B Twiss and Bruce Grelle, Westview Press, Boulder CO., 1998.
23 Psalms 104: 13-14 and 27-28.
24 Job 38:39-41.

and soul, then I will send rain for your land in season, both autumn and spring rains, and you will gather your corn and new wine and oil, and I will provide for your cattle: you shall eat your fill. Take good care not to be led astray in your hearts nor to turn aside and serve other gods and prostrate yourselves to them, or the Lord will become angry with you: he will shut up the skies and there will be no rain, your ground will not yield its harvest, and you will soon vanish from the rich land which the Lord is giving you.[25]

The Hebrew Scriptures and the Rabbinic tradition show deep concern for both the environment and for the welfare of animals. The Sabbath rest applies to animals as well as humans and the land has its Sabbath every seven years when it should be left fallow. During war, fruit-bearing trees are not to be destroyed.[26] In a comment on this verse the mystical Zohar says, "If you cut down a tree before its time, it is as if you have destroyed a living soul".[27] Armies are also instructed to dispose of human excrement by burying it.[28]

The importance of trees is recognized and the New Year of the Trees (*Tu B'Sh'vat)* is celebrated by the planting of saplings. Adam is told by God to care for the trees. "See my works, how fine and excellent they are! Now all that I created was created for you. Think about this and do not harm or desolate the world: for if you harm it, there will be none to fix it after you".[29]

Critics, however, have suggested that Genesis 1:28 in which

---

25 Deuteronomy 11:13-17.
26 Deuteronomy 20:19-20.
27 Lewis G Regenstein, *Replenish the Earth,* SCM Press, 1991, p.187.
28 Deuteronomy 23:13.
29 In the Rabbinic Koheleth Rabbah, 7, 28.

God tells human beings to "subdue" the earth and "have dominion" over the fish and birds and animals, is partly responsible for Western (Christian) civilization's exploitation of both the natural world and animal life. The previous verse, however, says that men and women are created in the image of God, so God's intention is that they rule the earth and animal life in the same caring way that God rules over the world. It is also made clear that human beings are stewards and do not have an absolute possession of the earth. There are many passages in Scripture and in Rabbinical writings that give instruction about kindness to animals.

For Jesus and the early Christians, the Hebrew Scriptures were their Bible and they inherited its teaching. Jesus spoke of God's care for the sparrow and of the beauty of lilies of the field. Many early saints had a close rapport with nature and the animal creation. But Christianity has quite often been blamed for the environmental crisis and the emphasis of those Christian theologians who deal seriously with environmental concerns is usually one of repentance. They recognize that Biblical teaching has been forgotten or ignored and that the Enlightenment views, especially of Descartes, which regarded animals as little more than machines, have become dominant in the West.[30] Animals have been exploited in factory farming and for medical research. The natural world has also been exploited for profit. Gradually Christian thinkers are recovering the Biblical viewpoint and a concern for eco-justice or "environmental justice" is growing, but some Christians are so concerned to address the injustices from which human beings suffer that they do not give the necessary attention to environmental issues. Many more in the West are reluctant to alter their life style to meet the demands of the environmental crisis.

Islam, like the other Abrahamic religions, sees God as the sole Creator of all that exists and that God's creation has a purpose and a design. "To Him, belong all (creatures) in the heavens and on earth".[31]

---

30 Kusumita Pedersen, "Environmental Ethics in Perspective." See also *Replenish the Earth*, pp.78-9.
31 Qur'an, 21, 19.

Every detail is the result of God's will. God is the sole owner of all that is and human beings are God's stewards. Human behavior should be consistent with the unity and integrity of nature, preserving the earth and its resources for future generations. Many traditions or *Hadith*, give examples of the Prophet Muhammad's kindness to animals, his close relation to Nature and his simple style of life.

Bahai's also see the natural world as evidence of the goodness of God. "Not a single atom in the entire universe can be found which doth not declare the evidences of His might, which doth not glorify His holy name".[32] Both Baha'u'llah, the founder of the Baha'i religion, and his son, Abdu'l-Baha, urged human beings to show kindness to animals. Abdu'l-Baha wrote, "Tenderness and loving-kindness (to animals) are basic principles of God's heavenly kingdom".[33] The Sikh scriptures also see God's glory and mercy reflected in the natural world.

> *Merciful, merciful is the Lord.*
> *Merciful is my master.*
> *He blesses all beings with His bounties.*[34]

The sacredness of all life

In Hinduism, Buddhism and Jainism, the emphasis is on the continuity and sacredness of all life. There are stories about the Buddha's previous lives, some of which were as an animal. The Dalai Lama has said, "As a boy studying Buddhism, I was taught the importance of a caring attitude toward the environment. Our practice of non-violence applies not just to human beings but to all sentient beings".[35] In the Hindu Vaishnavite tradition, "The evolution of life on this planet is symbolized

---

32 Robert A White, "Spiritual Foundations for an Ecologically Sustainable Society", *Journal of Baha'i Studies*, 1.2.89.
33 *Replenish the Earth*, pp.262-63.
34 *Guru Granth Sahib*, p.724.
35 *Earth and Faith*, p.61.

by a series of divine incarnations (of Vishnu) beginning with fish, moving through amphibious forms and mammals, and then on into human incarnations. This view clearly holds that man did not spring fully formed to dominate the lesser life forms, but rather evolved out of these forms, and is therefore integrally linked to the whole of creation".[36] In Hinduism, souls are eternal and travel through an endless cycle of rebirths, until they attain *moksa* or liberation. In some traditions, it is held that these births may be as an animal. The Laws of Manu say that "Men who delight in doing hurt become carnivorous animals, those who eat forbidden foods, worms; thieves, creatures consuming their own kind. For stealing grain, a man becomes a rat". [37]

In Hinduism, mountains, rocks, trees and rivers as well as the Earth itself are regarded as sacred and may be addressed in worship. In the Vedas there are beautiful hymns to the Earth and to the Dawn. Let these verses serve as examples:

> *Impart to us those vitalizing forces*
> *That come, O Earth, from deep within your body,*
> *Your central point, your navel; purify us wholly.*
> *The Earth is mother; I am son of Earth.*
> *The Rain-giver is my father; may he shower on us blessings!*[38]

> *Dawn, the glorious bringer of graces, shines forth*
> *And flings wide open for us her shining doors.*
> *Stirring the whole world she displays her riches,*
> *Raising to consciousness all living creatures.*

> *She wakes to action all who repose in slumber.*
> *Some rise to labor for wealth, others to worship.*
> *Those who saw little before now see more clearly.*
> *Dawn raises to consciousness all living creatures.* [39]

---

36 From the Hindu Assisi Declaration by Dr Karan Singh, reprinted in *Earth and Faith*, p.10.
37 *The Laws of Manu*, vol 25 of *Sacred Books of the East*, trans. George Buhler, Clarendon Press, Oxford 1886, 496-98.
38 *The Vedic Experience*, Ed. Raimundo Panikkar, Darton, Longman and Todd, 1977, p.124.
39 *The Vedic Experience*, p.16.

It is Jains who most strongly emphasize the sacredness of all life. Even trees, vegetables, lichens, and seeds are thought to have souls. When freed from matter, these souls, in their pure state rise to the top of the universe where, along with other liberated souls, they are perfect and all-knowing, with infinite power and bliss.[40]

Jains also are the most rigorous in avoiding taking life. Almost all Jains are strict vegetarians, but a Jain monk wears a mask over his mouth to avoid swallowing an insect by mistake and sweeps the path before he walks on it so as not accidentally to crush an ant or beetle. When a tour group I was leading visited the beautiful Jain temple city of Shatrunjaya, we were not allowed to wear or carry anything made of leather and we were not allowed to take any food with us. Certainly there was an amazing sense of purity, holiness and peace on the holy mountain.

Mahatma Gandhi, who was born and grew up in Gujarat, where Jains are very influential, may have been influenced by Jainism in developing his teaching of *ahimsa* or non-violence. In advocating concern for all living beings, Gandhi especially emphasized "Cow Protection". "This," he said "is one of the most wonderful phenomena in all human evolution; for it takes the human being beyond his species ... Man through the cow is enjoined to realize his identity with all that lives. 'Cow Protection' is the gift of Hinduism to the world".[41]

Although animals in India are often treated with callousness or cruelty, Jains have set up animal sanctuaries in many places. The emphasis on non-violence is related to the ascetic tradition of renunciation in Hinduism, Buddhism and Jainism which we have already noticed.

Chinese religions also stress the unity of all life. The universe is seen as a single, living unity composed of a primal material force or *ch'i*. Heaven and Earth are looked upon as the parent of all things. Chang Tsai, in the eleventh century, beautifully expressed this in the 'Western

---

40 *Replenish the Earth*, p.231.
41 See my *What Can We Learn from Hinduism*, O Books, John Hunt Publishing, 2002, p.89.

Inscription.' He said:

> Heaven is my father and Earth is my
> mother, and even such a small creature as I
> finds an intimate place in their midst.
> Therefore that which fills the universe I
> regard as my body and that which directs
> the universe I consider as my nature. All
> people are my brothers and sisters, and all
> things my companions. [42]

Shinto religion also has a close affinity to nature. The Way of the *kami* sees a numinous presence or *kami* or "gods" in trees and rivers and rocks. The beauty of nature is seen as an experience of the sacred and Shinto temples are usually built in places of great beauty.

Native American religions and also African religions have a great sense of the sacredness of the Earth and of all living beings. In the well known words attributed to Chief Sealth (also known as Chief Seattle) of the Suquamish in 1854:

> *Every part of this Earth is sacred to my people.*
> *every shining pine needle,*
> *every sandy shore,*
> *every mist in the dark woods,*
> *every clearing and humming insect*
> *is holy in the memory and experience of my people.*[43]

Points of agreement

Despite the difference between those religions which see the natural world as the handiwork of God and those who stress the unity of all life,

---

42 *Source Book in Chinese Philosophy*, Princeton University, 1963, p.497.
43 Quoted in *Celebrating Earth Holy Days*, ed Susan J Clark, Crossroad 1992, p.114.

religious traditions, as Dr Kusumita Pedersen has suggested, to a greater or lesser extent, agree on the following points:

The natural world has value in itself, and does not exist solely to serve human needs.

There is significant continuity of being between human and non-human living beings, even though humans do have a distinctive role. This continuity can be felt and experienced.

Non-human living beings are morally significant, in the eyes of God and/or in the cosmic order. They have unique relations to God, and their own places in the cosmic order.

The dependence of human life on the natural world can and should be acknowledged in ritual and other expressions of appreciation and gratitude.

Moral norms such as justice, compassion and reciprocity apply (in appropriate ways) both to human beings and to non-human beings. The well-being of humans and the well-being of non-human beings are inseparably connected.

There are legitimate and illegitimate uses of nature.

Greed and destructiveness are condemned. Restraint and protection are commended.

Human beings are obliged to be aware and responsible in living in harmony with the natural world, and should follow the specific practices for this prescribed by their traditions. [44]

Besides this theoretical consensus, which is very significant, there is a great deal of practical interfaith work both in protecting the environment, caring for the animal creation and ensuring that all people have the basic necessities of life. Many faith communities now have organizations which concentrate on environmental issues. There are also international organizations in which the faiths are working together and contributing to national and international efforts to protect the

---

44 Kusumita Pedersen, "Environmental Ethics in Perspective". Reproduced in *Earth and Faith*, p.78

environment through, for example, the Interfaith Partnership for the Environment, which works with the United Nations Environment Program, The Alliance of Religions and Conservation, the Forum on Religion and Ecology and the Earth Charter Campaign.

A compelling vision

The bigger question however, is, can religions provide a vision which is so compelling that it motivates not only people of faith but humanity as a whole to take the action which is essential if the worst dangers of the environmental crisis are to be averted? People of faith need to work with people in many other disciplines, but inter-religious dialogue has a crucial role to play as we re-invent ourselves, because it brings together the whole store of ethical resources that religions have to help us grapple with the crisis. "Earth's distress, after all, is the most ecumenical of issues. As such it requires a religious response of corresponding scope. No one religious tradition will suffice. Religions altogether will not save the planet, for that matter. Yet neither will the earth be saved without them".[45]

It has to be admitted that whatever their teaching, many faith communities have not been very successful in persuading their followers to reverence the earth and to care for the animal creation. Examples of ill treatment of living beings and of ecological degradation can, sadly, be found in many parts of the world. Followers of most faiths fall short of their ideals, but have faith leaders given the necessary priority to this issue? It is said that "a primary component of the Earth Charter initiative is a process of values internalization by millions of individuals, generating public awareness and the necessary change towards a better future".[46] Faith communities could play a large part in helping to internalize earth-friendly values.

---

45 Larry L Rasmussen, *Earth Community, Earth Ethics,* Orbis Books, 1996, p.271.
46 Quoted in *Threshold 2000,* p.155.

There is, however, the further difficulty that, just as faiths do not have a ready-made answer to the problems of globalization, equally the complexities of the current environmental crisis are new. Traditional teaching often presupposed a static and local society and much of the teaching was addressed to the individual. Dr Pedersen writes, "We have been taught to 'repent', but we have not been taught to 're-invent'".[47] Father Thomas Berry, a leading environmental theologian, insists that religions have to recognize that that "the universe is now experienced as an irreversible time-developmental process ... Not so much a cosmos as a cosmogenesis".[48] This implies that human beings are co-creators with God. For weal or woe, the future is in human hands. "The first great contribution this new perspective makes to religious consciousness," writes Father Berry, "is the sense of participating in the creation process itself. We bear within us the impress of every transformation through which the universe and the planet have passed".[49] This also means that human beings have to see themselves as part of the earth community and recognize that all life is bound together.

Perhaps it is only as we recognize our inter-connectedness with all life that we shall find a vision to motivate us. Pictures of the earth taken from space have provided such a vision for some people and have been called a symbol for our age. Astronauts David Brown and Kalpana Chawla, who both died in the Columbia spacecraft disaster, spoke of the magical beauty of our planet as seen from space. "If I'd been born in space," David Brown said, "I would desire to visit beautiful Earth more than I ever yearned to visit space. It's a wonderful planet". Kalpana Chawla said, "The first view of Earth is magical ... in such a small planet, with such a small ribbon of life, so much goes on. You get the feeling that I need to work extraordinarily hard along with other human beings to respect that".[50]

---

47 Kusumita Pedersen "Environmental Ethics in Perspective".
48 Dr Thomas Berry, "The Cosmology of Religions", in *A Source Book for Earth's Community of Religions*, CoNexus Press, 1995 edition, p.95.
49 "The Cosmology of Religions", p.96.
50 Quoted in Marcus Braybrooke, *365 Meditations for a Peaceful Heart and a Peaceful World*, Godsfield Press, 2004, p.380.

Mystics who have explored inner space proclaim the same message of unity. The French Jesuit and paleontologist Teilhard de Chardin said, "I live at the heart of a single, unique Element, the Centre of the Universe, and present in each part of it; personal Love and cosmic Power".[51] Fr. Thomas Berry has written, "We are earthlings. The Earth is our origin, our nourishment, our support, our guide. Our spirituality itself is Earth-derived".[52] As the environmentalist Jane Goodall says, "We are moving toward the ultimate destiny of our species – a state of compassion and love".[53]

It is an awareness of our oneness with all life and with the Source of Being that will inspire our compassion and energy to rediscover the way to live in harmony with nature, ensuring that it is protected for future generations and that all beings are valued and their right to life is respected. To share in shaping such an earth community in which all life is held precious is today's exciting and challenging call to faith and commitment.

---

51 Teilhard de Chardin, quoted in "'The Cosmology of Religions", p.97,
52 Thomas Berry quoted in "The Cosmology of Religions", p. 98. See also, Thomas Berry, "The Spirituality of the Earth" in *Celebrating Earth Holy Days*, Ed. Susan J Clark, Crossroad, 1992, pp.69-82.
53 Jane Goodall, *Reason for Hope*, Warner Books, 1999, p.267.

CONCLUSION

"A Civilization with a Heart" is the beautiful name that Wayne Teasdale, a prophet of inter-spirituality, gives to the alternative global future.[1] It will be a world in which every life is held precious and therefore a society committed to non-violence, economic co-operation and reverence for planet earth. It will be a society which embodies the mystic or unitive vision of inter-connectedness and the sacredness of all beings in the Divine.

In all the great spiritual traditions, there are pointers to such a civilization with a heart and there is also evidence in many places of an emerging global and spiritual consciousness. At the same time, the media reports escalating violence, growing economic inequality and ever-greater threats to the environment.

I believe the great spiritual traditions offer us an alternative to the gloom-laden predictions of popular pundits. All people of faith need now to concentrate together on proclaiming and living the alternative vision. It is our choice and our responsibility. As co-creators of the future, with the Divine Energy, we are called to provide a Heart for the world. In this book I have tried to envisage practical policies that flow from this vision: but the most important challenge to each of us as individuals is to shape our lives so that already we live as members of that civilization or, in the words of Mairead Maguire, the Irish Nobel Peace Prize Winner, "Dream the impossible, then so live that the dream is fulfilled".[2]

---

1 Wayne Teasdale, *The Mystic Heart*, New World Library, 1999. On pp.4-7 he mentions signs of the inter-spiritual age, which together are preparing for "a civilization with a heart".
2 Mairead Corrigan Maguire, *The Vision of Peace*, Orbis Books, 1999.

Appendix 1

WELCOME AND UNWELCOME TRUTHS BETWEEN JEWS, CHRISTIANS AND MUSLIMS

A PLATFORM STATEMENT FROM THE STERNBERG CENTRE JCM DIALOGUE GROUP

Unwelcome truths

While rejecting the widespread notion that religion is always and necessarily divisive, we believe that Jews, Christians and Muslims should acknowledge some unwelcome truths:

1. At various times in history relations between the three communities have been marred by discrimination and violence, and within each community religion has also been a source of sectarian strife.

2. In Jewish, Christian and Muslim scriptures and traditions one can find passages that have often been interpreted to support exclusive truth claims and a sense of superiority.

3. In practice, each faith has been notably self-centered and lacking in self-criticism, claiming for itself a superior position and a unique authority. Humility has often been notably lacking, and in its place arrogance and triumphalism have been all too evident.

The danger

There is a real danger now that these unwelcome truths, combined with political injustice, human rights abuses, poverty, hatred, fear, ignorance, globalization, war as an instrument of imperial policy, and the failure to respect international legal or ethical principles, will aggravate conflicts, intolerance, and even anarchy around the world.

The remedy

Jews, Christians and Muslims must not allow their religion to be abused in this way by exclusivist ideologues. We must make a stand together for peace, understanding, compassion and justice. We must welcome religious diversity and concede that no single religion can claim a monopoly of Truth. We must each put our own house in order, recognizing what we have in common, accepting that our scriptures and histories are interconnected, and acknowledging our interdependence. Each faith has its contribution to make both separately and together: indeed, at this era in history we need each other far more than in the past, and the future of our world demands that we teach to our communities the value and benefits of dialogue, co-operation and interdependence.

Welcome truths

Jews, Christians and Muslims can be inspired to change their mind-sets for the better by considering the following welcome truths:

1. We worship and serve the God who created and sustains the universe, the One God of Abraham, Moses, Jesus, and Muhammad. Behind our differences lies One unity.

2. We share the same general code of ethics, which condemns murder, theft and adultery, and demands that we secure the rights of those who have been denied their rights, to care for those in need, the sick, the suffering, the widow and the orphan, to welcome the stranger, the outcast and the persecuted, and to offer shelter and refuge to the homeless and the dispossessed.

3. Each of us inherits a broad and rich religious tradition within which many different views can coexist.

What we believe

We believe that:

1. Religious and cultural diversity should be valued and celebrated, in the full knowledge that each faith tradition is unique and invaluable.

2. As human beings with human limitations, we will never be able to grasp the full meaning of the Truth or comprehend God's nature.

3. Our respective religious traditions are capable of exploring the implications of new insights and dilemmas presented by modern science and technology and that we have a duty to reinterpret our religion with this aim in mind.

4. Our religious scriptures must not be used in a simplistic way; they need careful interpretation, bearing in mind both their historical context and their relevance to present needs.

5. Our religious traditions can best flourish in just, pluralistic and democratic societies, where there is freedom of worship and where the rights of all individuals are respected.

6. Missionary work that provokes antagonism and resentment should be strongly discouraged.

7. God is the true Owner of everything, that we are finite, and that all that we have is a loan or gift from God; we therefore have a duty to look after this planet and protect its natural resources and its variety of interdependent life forms, for the sake of future generations.

8. The sanctity of all life is defiled by war, terrorism, genocide, torture, rape, extra-judicial killings, and detention without trial.

9. Scripture should not be used to justify violence, oppression, exploitation, military aggression or claims of superiority

10. That which binds us to God also binds us to one another as a single human family.

What needs to be done?

1. There is a desperate need for education in Judaism, Christianity and Islam. Too many are ignorant of the teachings of their own faith, and

know even less about the other faiths. Our day schools and religious institutions have a duty to teach not only adherence to our own traditions but also knowledge of other traditions, placing special emphasis on the ethical aspects and what they have in common.

2. Through school programs and the mass media, social harmony should be promoted by making us more aware of the contribution to civilization made by other religions, cultures and civilizations.

3. Jews, Christians and Muslims should work together as equal partners. Equal respect and theological space should be accorded to each faith. A just and peaceful world can only be achieved in partnership.

4. Jewish, Christian and Muslim scholars should be made more aware of their duty to demonstrate how their sacred texts and religious traditions are relevant to current needs.

5. Since it is God's will that we should strive to become, as best we can, the servants of His love and compassion, we should seek to resolve disputes by means of forgiveness, empathy and reconciliation, and encourage others to do the same. We should all be able to answer affirmatively the question posed by the other: "Do you know what causes me pain?"

6. We should refute exclusivist perversions of Judaism, Christianity and Islam that glorify war and aggressive behavior, and we should condemn those who spread false stereotypes of the Other.

7. We, as Jews, Christians and Muslims, have a duty to challenge the misuse of power and to demand that governments tackle the roots of terrorism, using diplomacy as a first resort, with respect for human dignity, human rights and the due process of law. We have a duty to defend the right to asylum where this is wrongfully withheld, and to seek to abide by ethical and humanitarian principles both at home and abroad.

8. We have a duty to truth and reconciliation which demands of us that we recognize we are all the victims of different and irreconcilable accounts of current and past public events, and that only together can we build shared narratives based on accurate testimony and records.

We can only achieve our shared vision of a repaired and transformed world by pooling the best of our respective teachings and talents in partnership and shared endeavor. Only full and effective partnership can end conflict and bring peace, with opportunities to ponder together the wonder of creation and the mystery of God.

This statement was agreed by a group of Jews Christians and Muslims who have been meeting for twelve years, although some members joined more recently. The signatories are:

Jewish: Rabbi Tony Bayfield, Rabbi Michael Hilton, Rabbi Jonathan Magonet, Rabbi Elizabeth Tikvah Sarah, Rabbi Norman Solomon.

Christian: Revd Eric Allen, Revd John Bowden, Revd Marcus Braybrooke, Revd Alan Race, Dr Jenny Sankey.

Muslim: Mr Rumman Ahmed, Dr Roger Abdul Wahhab Boase, Imam Abduljalil Sajid, Dr Ataullah Siddiqui.

APPENDIX 2

The Millennium Development Goals

1. Eradicate extreme poverty and hunger.

   Halve, between 1990 and 2015, the proportion of people whose income is less than US$1 a day.

   Halve, between 1990 and 2015, the proportion of people who suffer from hunger.

2. Achieve universal primary education.

   Ensure that by 2015, children everywhere, boys and girls alike, will be able to complete a full course of primary schooling.

3. Promote gender equality and empower women.

   Eliminate gender disparity in primary and secondary education, preferably by 2005, and in all levels of education no later that 2015.

4. Reduce child mortality.

   Reduce by two thirds, between 1990 and 2015, the under-five mortality rate.

5. Improve maternal health.

   Reduce by three quarters, between 1990 and 2015, the maternal mortality rate.

6. Combat HIV/Aids, Malaria and other diseases.

   Have halted by 2015 and begun to reverse the spread of HIV/AIDS

   Have halted by 2015 and begun to reverse the incidence of malaria and other major diseases.

7. Ensure environmental sustainability.

Integrate the principle of sustainable development into country policies and programs and reverse the loss of environmental resources.

Halve by 2015 the proportion of people without sustainable access to safe drinking water.

Have achieved, by 2020, a significant improvement in the lives of at least 100 million slum dwellers.

8. Develop a Global Partnership for Development.

Develop further an open, rule-based, predictable non-discriminatory trading and financial system (includes a commitment to good governance, development, and poverty reduction – both nationally and internationally).

Address the special needs of the least developed countries (includes tariff – and quota-free access for exports, enhanced program of debt relief for and cancellation of official bilateral debt, and more generous official development assistance to countries committed to poverty reduction)

Address the special needs of landlocked countries and small island developing states (through the Program for Action for the Sustainable Development of Small Island Developing States and the 22nd General Assembly provisions).

Deal comprehensively with debt problems of developing countries through national and international measures in order to make debts sustainable in the long term.

In co-operation with developing countries, develop and implement strategies for decent and productive work for youth.

In co-operation with pharmaceutical companies, provide access to affordable essential drugs in developing countries.

In co-operation with the private sector, make available the benefits of new technologies, especially information and communication technologies.

These Millennium Development Goals were established at the United Nations Millennium Summit in September 2000.

Appendix 3

'The Gift of Water'

An Interfaith Celebration

Introduction

Sung Invocation

> *Come, come, whoever you are,*
> *Wanderer, worshipper, lover of leaving,*
> *Ours is no caravan of despair,*
> *Come, yet again, come.*
> *(words by Rumi)*

Water is essential for life. Water is also a universal symbol, although different sacred traditions emphasize special aspects of the spiritual significance of water. In 1993, at the start of celebrations to mark the centenary of the first World Parliament of Religions, members of different faiths brought water from holy rivers, such as the Ganges and the Jordan, to signify our longing to cleanse and revive the earth and to wash away prejudice and suffering.

In this observance, we shall first reflect on the symbolism of water in some of our sacred traditions – but there is only time for a small selection. Then we shall think of the many families who do not have access to clean water, which should be the birthright of every child. Finally we shall take time to consider what we can do individually or in our own community to ensure that all people enjoy this precious gift of

God and we shall be invited to share in a simple act of commitment. Please join in the songs if you wish.

Part 1: The symbolism of water in the sacred traditions

In some traditions, creation itself begins with water.

1. The Bible opens with these words:

> In the beginning God created the heaven and the earth. And the earth was without form, and void and darkness was upon the face of the deep. And the Spirit of God moved upon the face of the waters. (Genesis 1:1-2 AV)

2. The Vedas say

> Of this Universe, in truth the Waters were made first. Hence when the waters flow, then everything here, whatsoever exists is produced. (Satapatha Brahmana XII, 5, 2, 14)

All life depends on water

3. The Psalmist says:

> You visit the earth and water it: you greatly enrich it with the river of God, which is full of water: you prepare corn for them … You water the ridges abundantly and make it soft with showers: you bless the springing thereof. (Psalms 65:10-11)

We use water to wash and make ourselves physically clean. In many traditions water is also used symbolically of being made spiritually clean.

4. The Qur'an says

> O you who believe, when you prepare for prayer, wash your faces and your hands and your arms to the elbows. Rub your heads with water and wash your feet to your ankles. (Qur'an 5, 6)

5. In the Shinto tradition, the purification ceremony of Misogi may involve standing beneath a waterfall.

6. In the Sikh tradition, at the Amrit ceremony, water with sugar crystals is used

> Guru Nanak compared the soul's thirst for God to a fish's longing for water.
>
> Oh my mind, love God as a fish loves water:
> The more the water, the happier is the fish,
> The more peaceful his mind and body.
> He cannot live without water even for a moment.
> God knows the inner pain of being without water.

In some traditions the crossing of water is a symbol of salvation. Water represents painful existence in the world. Tossed about on the turbulent sea, the wayfarer finds rest or Nirvana only on the other shore. In other traditions, death is seen as crossing a river to a new life.

7. From the Jain Scriptures:

> The body, they say, is a boat and the soul is the sailor. Samsara is the ocean which is crossed by the great sages. (Uttaradhyana Sutra 23, 73)

8. From the Buddhist scriptures

> Few are there among men who go across to the further shore; the rest of humankind only run about on the bank. But those who act rightly according to the teaching, as has been well taught, will cross over to the other shore, for the realm of passions is so difficult to cross. (Dhammapada 85-6)

Pause now to reflect on these images. In different ways water has suggested to people images of healing and wholeness. Picture yourself being washed clean - your worries and fears being taken away or picture yourself reaching the far shore of peace. As you are healed and become peaceful – peace flows out to others.

Song: 'Peace is flowing like a river.'

> Peace is flowing like a river,
> Flowing out through you and me,
> Spreading out into the desert,
> Setting all the people free.
>
> Love is flowing like a river
> Flowing out through you and me,
> Spreading out into the desert,
> Setting all the people free.
>
> Joy is flowing like a river
> Flowing out through you and me,
> Spreading out into the desert,
> Setting all the people free.
>
> Hope is flowing like a river
> Flowing out through you and me,
> Spreading out into the desert,
> Setting all the people free.
> (Words and music traditional)

Part II: Water should be a symbol of compassion and of justice and of our responsibility to treasure the environment.

9. Compassion
Sadly, over a billion people do not have access to clean water. Each year about 2.2 million children die of dehydration caused by diarrhoea - most of those who die are under two years of age.

The World Health Organisation reckons that 90% of these children could be saved by prevention or better treatment.

Jesus said:

> *If anyone gives even a cup of cold water to one of these little ones,*
> *I tell you the truth, he will not lose his reward.*
> *(Matthew 10:42).*

A story from Tanzania was read

10. Justice

Many people are victims of injustice. For example: of the 104 million children worldwide who don't go to school, many have to walk miles to collect water and have no time for school. Even then, the water may be of poor quality and cause illness.

Agnes Matibya from Tanzania says that before the village had water. "I couldn't wash my children's clothes very often, so they would get scabies a lot. They also suffered from malaria and diarrhea often."

The Prophet Amos said:

Let justice roll on like a river, righteousness like a never-failing stream. (Amos 5:24)

11. Treasure the Environment

Massive pollution of the world's surface water systems has placed a great strain on supplies of clean fresh water. Global deforestation, destruction of wetlands, dumping of pesticides and fertilizer into waterways are all taking a terrible toll on Earth's fragile water systems.

The Native American tradition reminds us

> If we lose the sweetness of the waters, we lose the life of the land,
> If we lose the life of the land, we lose the majesty of the forest,
> If we lose the majesty of the forest, we lose the purity of the air,
> If we lose the purity of the air, we lose the creatures of the Earth.

Song: When I needed a neighbor.

When I needed a neighbor, were you there, were you there?
When I needed a neighbor were you there?
Chorus: And the creed and the color and the name won't matter,
Were you there?

I was hungry and thirsty, were you there, were you there?
I was hungry and thirsty, were you there?
Chorus: And the creed and the color and the name won't matter,
Were you there?

I was cold, I was naked, were you there, were you there?
I was cold, I was naked, were you there?
Chorus: And the creed and the color and the name won't matter,
Were you there?

When I needed a shelter, were you there, were you there?
When I needed a shelter, were you there?
Chorus: And the creed and the color and the name won't matter,
Were you there?

When I needed a healer, were you there, were you there?
When I needed a healer, were you there?
Chorus: And the creed and the color and the name won't matter,
Were you there?

Wherever you travel, I'll be there, I'll be there?
Wherever you travel, I'll be there, I'll be there?

Chorus: And the creed and the color and the name won't matter,
Were you there?

Words and music: Sydney Carter

Part III: What can we do?

Consider our life style. How concerned are we for the environment?
Give to help those who do not have good water.
Campaign to ensure governments meet UN targets.

*Reflect in silence on what you intend to do when you get home. You
may like to tell your neighbor.*

Song: The Pilgrims' Hymn
We ask that we live and labor in peace, in peace.
Each one shall be our neighbor, in peace, in peace.
Distrust and hatred will turn to love, All the pris'ners freed
And our only war will be the one
Against all human need.

We work for the end of disunion in truth, in truth;
That all may be one communion in truth, in truth;
We choose the road of peace and prayer
Countless pilgrims trod,
So that Hindu, Muslim Christian, Jew,
We all can worship one God.

We call to our sisters and brothers, unite, unite!
That all may live for others, unite, unite!
And so the nations will be as one,
One the flag unfurled,
One law, one faith, one hope, one truth,
One people and one world.

Words and music: Donald Swann.

This interfaith celebration was arranged by the World Congress of
Faiths at the 2004 Parliament of World Religions in Barcelona.

O

is a symbol of the world,
of oneness and unity. O Books
explores the many paths of wholeness
and spiritual understanding which
different traditions have developed down
the ages. It aims to bring this knowledge
in accessible form, to a general readership,
providing practical spirituality to today's seekers.

For the full list of over 200 titles covering:

- CHILDREN'S PRAYER, NOVELTY AND GIFT BOOKS
- CHILDREN'S CHRISTIAN AND SPIRITUALITY
- CHRISTMAS AND EASTER
- RELIGION/PHILOSOPHY
- SCHOOL TITLES
- ANGELS/CHANNELLING
- HEALING/MEDITATION
- SELF-HELP/RELATIONSHIPS
- ASTROLOGY/NUMEROLOGY
- SPIRITUAL ENQUIRY
- CHRISTIANITY, EVANGELICAL
  AND LIBERAL/RADICAL
- CURRENT AFFAIRS
- HISTORY/BIOGRAPHY
- INSPIRATIONAL/DEVOTIONAL
- WORLD RELIGIONS/INTERFAITH
- BIOGRAPHY AND FICTION
- BIBLE AND REFERENCE
- SCIENCE/PSYCHOLOGY

Please visit our website,
www.O-books.net